TECHNICAL REPORT

Aligning Post-Secondary Educational Choices to Societal Needs

A New Scholarship System for Qatar

Catherine H. Augustine • Cathy Krop

Prepared for the Supreme Education Council

RAND RAND-QATAR POLICY INSTITUTE

The research described in this report was prepared for the Supreme Education Council and conducted within the RAND-Qatar Policy Institute and RAND Education, programs of the RAND Corporation.

Library of Congress Cataloging-in-Publication Data

Augustine, Catherine H., 1968-
Aligning post-secondary educational choices to societal needs : a new scholarship system for Qatar / Catherine H. Augustine, Cathy Krop.
p. cm.
Includes bibliographical references.
ISBN 978-0-8330-4420-4 (pbk. : alk. paper)
1. Scholarships—Qatar. 2. Education, Higher—Aims and objectives—Qatar. I. Krop, Cathy S. (Cathy Sloan), 1966– II. Title.

LB2339.Q2A94 2008
378.3'4095363—dc22

2008015237

The RAND Corporation is a nonprofit research organization providing objective analysis and effective solutions that address the challenges facing the public and private sectors around the world. RAND's publications do not necessarily reflect the opinions of its research clients and sponsors.

Cover photograph courtesy of Supreme Education Council

Published 2008 by the RAND Corporation
1776 Main Street, P.O. Box 2138, Santa Monica, CA 90407-2138
1200 South Hayes Street, Arlington, VA 22202-5050
4570 Fifth Avenue, Suite 600, Pittsburgh, PA 15213-2665
RAND URL: http://www.rand.org/
To order RAND documents or to obtain additional information, contact
Distribution Services: Telephone: (310) 451-7002;
Fax: (310) 451-6915; Email: order@rand.org

Preface

Since the 1970s, Qatar has had a scholarship system designed to send students abroad for undergraduate and graduate programs not available locally. In 2003, the Supreme Education Council (SEC) requested that the RAND Corporation provide recommendations on reforming the system. The SEC specified that a new scholarship system for Qatar should complement and promote its national K–12 reforms, utilize the expanding high-quality post-secondary options available in the country, and meet the labor-related, civic, and cultural needs generated from Qatar's significant economic and social development.

RAND developed recommendations to improve Qatar's scholarship system and provided the SEC with a final project report at the end of 2003. The SEC accepted these recommendations and, in September 2004, established the Higher Education Institute (HEI), with a similar organizational structure and functions to those of RAND's proposed Post-Secondary Education Institute. The HEI has adopted the goals and principles suggested in this report, along with most of RAND's recommendations on scholarship programs. That said, it has also transformed and improved upon our ideas and suggestions. We are grateful to have had the opportunity to conduct this study, which has helped to launch what has become a prominent and important institute in Qatar.

This report summarizes our evaluation of the old system and our resulting recommendations. This research should be of interest to policymakers in other wealthy countries balancing support for in-country post-secondary institutions with support for students to study abroad.

The RAND-Qatar Policy Institute and RAND Education

This project was conducted under the auspices of the RAND-Qatar Policy Institute (RQPI) and RAND Education. RQPI is a partnership of the RAND Corporation and the Qatar Foundation for Education, Science, and Community Development. The aim of RQPI is to offer the RAND style of rigorous and objective analysis to clients in the greater Middle East. In serving clients in the Middle East, RQPI draws on the full professional resources of the RAND Corporation. RAND Education analyzes education policy and practice and supports the implementation of improvements at all levels of the education system.

For further information on RQPI, contact the director, Richard Darilek. He can be reached by email at rqpi@rand.org; by telephone at +974-492-7400; or by mail at P.O. Box 23644, Doha, Qatar. For more information about RAND Education, contact the associate director, Charles Goldman. He can be reached by email at Charles_Goldman@rand.org; by telephone at +1-310-393-0411, extension 6748; or by mail at RAND, 1776 Main Street, Santa Monica, California 90401 USA.

Contents

Figures

Tables

Summary

Since 1995, the Emir of Qatar, Sheikh Hamad bin Khalifa al-Thani, has led the country on a course of significant economic and social development. This development demands that Qatar's population acquire specialized technical skills, competency in English and other languages,[1] critical-thinking and problem-solving skills, leadership experience, and the capability to operate in an international environment. Post-secondary study is an essential means to acquiring these skills and, in turn, to producing a highly skilled labor force.

Pursuant to a scholarship law issued in the 1970s, Qatar has supported study abroad in undergraduate and graduate programs not available locally. Although the law has not been updated since the 1970s, the country has undergone major societal shifts since then. Workforce needs have evolved, and there are increasing demands for Qataris in the labor force. Recently, Qatar has made substantial investments in primary- and secondary-education reforms and in the expansion of in-country post-secondary options. Several highly selective post-secondary institutions have established branch campuses in the capital city of Doha, and Qatar University has undergone major reform. A scholarship system that includes post-secondary counseling, comprehensive recipient support, and widespread data collection and analysis would allow Qatar to capitalize on these educational reforms while developing the human capital it needs to support its economic and social development.

In 2003, the Supreme Education Council (SEC) of Qatar requested that RAND provide recommendations for improving the country's scholarship programs. Leaders of the country wanted to ensure that the scholarship system and the laws supporting it were aligned to the new workforce and post-secondary contexts. They also wanted suggestions on how to ensure that their investments in the scholarship programs generated returns in terms of students attending high-quality post-secondary institutions. In particular, they wanted to ensure that students who were studying abroad were enrolling in institutions of higher quality than those available in the country. The SEC asked us to consider all aspects of the system, including its purpose and outcomes, as well as processes (e.g., financing and contracting with students) and policies (e.g., student and institutional eligibility).

To understand the strengths and weaknesses of the then-current system, we conducted more than 50 interviews with stakeholders, including SEC members, scholarship sponsors, students, graduates, college officials, cultural attaché staff, and other student-support providers. RAND collected data on scholarship recipients, examining rankings of the colleges and universities they attended, and reviewed the original (1976) and proposed (2003) scholarship

[1] Although most employers interviewed for this study specified a desire for English-speaking employees, a few argued that they also needed their employees to speak French.

laws. In addition, RAND reviewed selected scholarship programs around the world, focusing on countries similar to Qatar with respect to size, wealth, and internal post-secondary infrastructure. To learn firsthand about an advanced government-sponsored scholarship system, members of the RAND team met with a variety of employers and government officials in Singapore, a similar country in terms of size, wealth, post-secondary infrastructure, and its desire to augment in-country options with targeted study-abroad opportunities.

Our analysis demonstrated that Qatar's then-current scholarship system had a number of weaknesses:

- No single organization coordinated and administered the three main scholarship programs operating in Qatar.
- Policies and procedures within and across individual scholarship programs were not coherently designed or consistently executed, and systematic information was nonexistent.
- Prior to college, students were not receiving guidance or preparation to attend high-quality institutions.
- The system provided few incentives to attend high-quality institutions.
- Support services for recipients were inadequate.
- Choices about resource allocation and post-secondary education were impeded by a lack of data and analysis on Qatari participation in post-secondary education.

The purpose of our study was to provide recommendations to remedy these weaknesses. We proposed a new system to improve decisionmaking at multiple levels about higher education, from students' enrollment decisions to the country's decisions on investing in post-secondary learning. The proposed system was designed to meet goals that were elicited from our interviews of more than 50 country leaders and other stakeholders of the scholarship system. The goals included meeting workforce needs; developing language, critical thinking, and problem-solving skills; preparing future leaders; providing international exposure and establishing ties to other countries; and meeting civic and cultural needs. Our recommendations were further guided by principles of quality, accountability, efficiency, flexibility, and support. These principles are based on those of prestigious scholarship programs around the world, and Qataris confirmed that they were important during our interviews.

We argued that, if scholarships are to play a critical role in the larger education system, a major reform of the prior scholarship system would be required. Scholarship reform can be effective only within the context of broader measures that

- assist secondary-school students in making decisions about post-secondary study that benefit themselves, employers, and the state
- establish incentives for secondary students to excel, gain admission to high-quality post-secondary institutions, and achieve at those institutions
- track and evaluate recipient performance
- improve investment in human resources by conducting comprehensive data collection and analysis on all Qataris engaged in post-secondary study
- assess the quality of all institutions attended by Qataris—at home and abroad.

Proposed Scholarship Programs

RAND proposed a scholarship system centered on three programs for undergraduate and graduate study, in Education City and abroad. Receipt of a scholarship would be conditional on acceptance to an eligible post-secondary institution. All Qatari citizens of any age who have completed secondary school would be eligible to apply to these three programs. Qatari noncitizen residents would be eligible for the loan-based program, and we recommended that employers decide whether to sponsor noncitizen residents. Domestic options, including Qatar University and the colleges in Education City, would be prioritized through multiple mechanisms.

Prestigious Scholarship Program. A prestigious scholarship program would introduce flexibility as an incentive and would reward exceptional performance at the secondary level. A select number of recipients would have the choice to enroll in any major or degree program worldwide and would have very limited postgraduation obligations if admitted to a highly selective college or university. Eligible institutions could include Education City universities, the top 50 U.S. universities, the top 10 UK universities, and the top five universities in other countries.

Employer-Sponsored Program. An employer-sponsored program would meet Qatar's workforce needs. Employer-sponsored participants would be required to gain acceptance to a college or university that is of higher quality than Qatar University.[2] For degree programs offered in Qatar, applicants would need to first apply to, and be rejected by, institutions in Education City before winning a scholarship to study abroad.

Loan-Based Program. A loan-based program would provide an additional option for students who prefer not to study under contract with an employer or who are not accepted to the prestigious scholarship or employer-sponsored programs. Loans would be awarded after an applicant is admitted to a university or college that is of higher quality than Qatar University. An incentive in the form of subsidized interest rates could be granted for study at Education City universities or for courses of study deemed national priorities.

Based on pass rates on the secondary-school exit exam, approximately two-thirds of Qatari secondary-school students are prepared to enter college immediately after secondary school and, if accepted to an eligible institution, would receive a scholarship upon graduation. Because other prospective scholarship applicants may not be adequately prepared for study at a highly competitive institution, we proposed a precollege grant for language or other academic preparation. Grants would be allocated for study at the Qatar Foundation's Academic Bridge Program and other domestic developmental programs, as well as foundation and language programs abroad, with preference given to students who choose domestic programs. Grant awards would cover only the cost of the tuition, not travel or living allowances, to encourage enrollment in domestic programs.

Because our recommendations prioritized domestic universities, it is possible that the number of Qataris completing degree programs abroad would decline upon implementation of this new system. Given that international exposure is an important goal of this proposed scholarship system, students would be able to apply for grants for tuition and living allowances to study abroad for a short period.

---

[2] At the time of this study, Qatar University had an open admission policy, and all Qatari citizens could attend free of charge.

Considering the stringent proposed criteria for scholarship awards, it is also possible that the number of scholarship recipients would decline in the short run. Students not eligible for a scholarship would have three options for subsidized post-secondary study: enrolling in Qatar University, applying for a study-abroad grant in conjunction with enrolling at Qatar University, or applying for a precollege grant as a means of advancing toward eligibility for a scholarship in subsequent years. Elevating award criteria is critical to system success in the long run, because it would ultimately motivate applicants to excel in secondary school and gain admission to high-quality institutions.

Proposed Organizational Structure

Establishing this ambitious system would require a new infrastructure. We recommended establishing a post-secondary education institute that would, in collaboration with the SEC, set direction and vision for policies and research related to post-secondary education in Qatar. This institute would do more than manage scholarships in Qatar—it would also plan for and monitor post-secondary education in Qatar. This institute would provide counseling so that Qataris could make educational choices that both match their interests and meet Qatar's needs. The institute would also house competitive, incentive-based scholarship programs to motivate secondary-school students to excel and, in turn, gain admission to high-quality institutions. Highly skilled graduates studying at these institutions would contribute to Qatar's social and economic development.

Figure S.1 presents the proposed structure for the new institute. We recommended that the Post-Secondary Education Institute (PEI) house an institutional standards office, a scholarship office, and a student resource center. This independent PEI would be subordinate to the SEC. It would not have any formal relationship with the Ministry of Education, and, thus, the Ministry of Education would no longer be involved in Qatar's scholarship system except as an employer.

We recommended that an institutional standards office evaluate in-country post-secondary institutions against their foreign counterparts and provide authorization and licensing for col-

Figure S.1
Organizational Structure for the Post-Secondary Education Institute and Its Offices

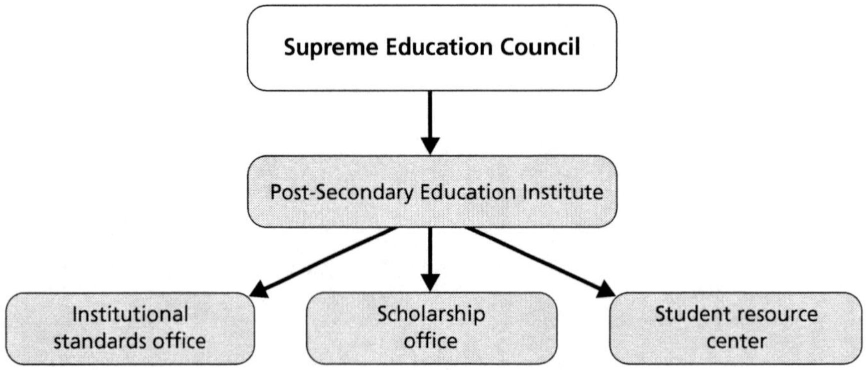

RAND *TR478-S.1*

leges to operate in Qatar. This office would strive to assess the educational quality of institutions and degree programs around the world and qualify institutions for each of the scholarship programs. Staff members would rely primarily on existing measures of institutional and degree-program quality, drawing on a body of secondary ranking sources.

A scholarship office would perform all functions related to the scholarship programs. Members of this office would propose policies, procedures, and scholarship guidelines that would, in turn, be approved by the director of the PEI and by the SEC. The guidelines would address qualifications for scholarship eligibility, English-language training options, and eligible countries, institutions, programs, and fields of study, including distance-learning options. Staff in this office would also design recipient contracts and financial packages, ensure that recipients fulfill all the obligations of their contracts—including meeting performance requirements—and interact with employers regarding labor-market needs. This office would be the point of contact for all scholarship recipients and alumni. Staff members would be responsible for assisting with visa applications and processing, hosting orientation events, providing ongoing support for students while they are in school, and reviewing requests for transfers and extensions.

While the scholarship office would support students who received scholarships, a student resource center would provide guidance to all Qataris interested in pursuing post-secondary education. A state-of-the-art student resource center could improve the quality of educational decisionmaking by ensuring that Qataris are studying at the best institutions for their abilities and for the country's needs. The center would assist Qataris of all ages with college preparation, applications, and degree-program and institution choice. Staff members could also conduct extensive outreach to secondary schools to provide academic and career counseling.

The SEC accepted these recommendations and, in September 2004, established the Higher Education Institute (HEI), with a similar organizational structure to the proposed PEI. The HEI critically assessed and adopted the goals and principles suggested in this report, along with many of our recommendations on scholarship programs. It has, in addition, transformed our ideas and suggestions in establishing an institute that is well suited to serve the country's needs. We are grateful to have had the opportunity to conduct this study, which has helped to launch what has become a prominent and important institute in Qatar.[3]

---

[3] Further information about the HEI and its current operations can be found in SEC (2008).

Acknowledgments

We are grateful to many people and organizations that provided valuable input at various stages of this project. Most importantly, we thank the members of the SEC in Qatar who guided our research and provided helpful feedback throughout its duration. We are also grateful to Adel Al-Sayed and Howaida Nadim for very thoughtful suggestions, as well as for support with the logistics of the interview and data-gathering processes. In addition, we would like to thank Jehan Al-Meer, former director of the HEI, for transforming the ideas and suggestions presented here into a prominent institute in Qatar and for providing comments on a draft of this report.

The following organizations in Qatar and elsewhere were very generous with their time and information: Academic Bridge Program, AMIDEAST (America–Middle East Educational and Training Services, Inc.), Center for Judicial and Legal Studies, College of the North Atlantic, Qatar's UK and U.S. cultural attaché offices, Hamad Medical Corporation, Institute for International Education, Kahramaa (Qatar General Electricity and Water Corporation), Ministry of Civil Services, Ministry of Education Scholarship Office, Ministry of Foreign Affairs, Ministry of Interior, Planning Council, Qatar Armed Forces, Qatar Foundation, Qatar Petroleum, Qatar University, Q-Tel (Qatar Telecom), Texas International Education Consortium, and Weill Cornell Medical School.

We would also like to thank Ministry of Education scholarship recipients in the United States and United Kingdom and Qatar Petroleum scholarship recipients in the United States for sharing their experiences and opinions about the scholarship system in Qatar. In addition, we thank Fatima Mohamed Al-Ali at Qatar Petroleum for helping us obtain to data on that organization's scholarship program and Sabri Mahmoud at the cultural attaché office in Washington, D.C., for data on Ministry of Education scholarship recipients in the United States.

Representatives from the following organizations in Singapore met with us to provide information on their scholarship programs: DBS Bank, Economic Development Board of Singapore, Public Service Commission of Singapore, Singapore Airlines, and Temasek Holdings.

At RAND, several people contributed to our analysis by reading through various drafts of the report or providing feedback on project briefings: Louay Constant, Julie DaVanzo, Susan Gates, Charles Goldman, Sheila Kirby, Richard C. Neu, Gery Ryan, Cathy Stasz, and Gail Zellman. We are grateful to Christopher Dirks and Donna White for editing and formatting, which greatly improved the presentation of this report.

Last, but certainly not least, we thank Tora Bikson and Marvin Peterson for reviewing this document. Their comments and suggestions greatly improved its content.

Abbreviations

AMIDEAST	America–Middle East Educational and Training Services, Inc.
GRE	Graduate Record Examination
HEI	Higher Education Institute
NIH	National Institutes of Health
OECD	Organization for Economic Co-Operation and Development
PEI	Post-Secondary Education Institute
PSC	Singapore Public Service Commission
QNEDS	Qatar National Education Data System
RQPI	RAND Qatar Policy Institute
SEC	Supreme Education Council
TOEFL	Test of English as a Foreign Language
VCU	Virginia Commonwealth University

CHAPTER ONE

Introduction

Context

The nation of Qatar is one of the smallest of the Arabian Gulf states.[1] Nonetheless, due to its oil and natural-gas reserves, it is one of the wealthiest countries in the world (with a per capita GDP of $29,800),[2] and, due to its leadership, it is one of the most progressive states in the gulf region. Qatar is experiencing unprecedented social and economic development, which is inextricably intertwined with increased participation in a competitive global environment. The Emir, Sheikh Hamad bin Khalifa al-Thani, is diversifying the economy with an emphasis on creating a vibrant private sector and increasing employment opportunities for Qatari nationals. This development demands specialized human capital. However, the Qatari population is small, and the country depends on a large expatriate workforce—not just for low-skilled labor, but for highly skilled labor as well. Few Qataris have the training or qualifications needed for high-demand, high-skill jobs (Stasz et al., 2007). *Qatarization* policies aim to increase Qatari employment in the private sector, as well as in the semiprivate energy sector. These policies will work only if Qataris are prepared to assume these positions, most of which require specific knowledge and skills (Stasz et al., 2007).

To support this rapid economic development, Qatar is committed to providing its citizens with the best education possible, both by increasing the quality of domestic options and by sending students abroad. Qatar's primary- and secondary-school system, comprised of approximately 300 schools and 90,000 students, is undergoing major reform that should lead to improved student outcomes.[3] At the post-secondary level, Education City now houses several high-quality foreign colleges and universities: Carnegie Mellon University, Georgetown Universitym, Texas A&M University, Virginia Commonwealth University (VCU), and Weill Cornell Medical College. The country's one public university, Qatar University, is aggressively reforming its admission standards, programmatic offerings, and administrative operations.

Since the 1970s, Qatar has complemented its in-country post-secondary options (which, until recently, were limited to Qatar University and VCU) by supporting citizens to study abroad in undergraduate and graduate programs not available locally. There were three main types of scholarship programs in Qatar supporting post-secondary study in 2003: Ministry of Education–sponsored, joint Ministry of Education– and employer-sponsored, and employer-sponsored. At any one time, approximately 1,000 Qatari students studied on Ministry of Edu-

---

[1] *Arabian Gulf* is the name used here for the body of water that some readers call the *Persian Gulf*.

[2] 2006 estimate from CIA (2007).

[3] See Brewer et al. (2007) for detailed information on K–12 reform in Qatar.

cation and jointly offered scholarships, both in-country and abroad, at both the undergraduate and graduate levels.[4] Historically, between 200 and 300 new scholarships were issued each year. Hundreds of additional students studied on employer-sponsored scholarships each year. When RAND was asked to conduct this study, there was no single organization coordinating and administering all three programs or ensuring that recipients attended universities that were appropriate for the students' and the country's needs.

Study Purpose and Audience

In 2003, Qatar's Supreme Education Council (SEC) requested that RAND provide recommendations on reforming the scholarship system. Qatari leaders have spearheaded several societal shifts since the scholarship law was first written in the 1970s. Workforce needs have changed, with increasing demands for Qataris in the labor force. In the post-secondary sector, several highly selective post-secondary institutions have established branch campuses in the capital city of Doha, and Qatar University has undergone major reform. The SEC wanted to ensure that the scholarship system was aligned with these workforce and post-secondary–sector changes. Moreover, the Qatari government wanted assurances that its investments in the scholarship system were not undermining or in conflict with its investments in post-secondary education more generally and that its citizens were able to attend high-quality colleges and universities, both at home and abroad. In particular, Qatar's leaders asked us to consider establishing a system through which students could study abroad only at institutions of higher quality than those available in the country. Moreover, they also expected that most students enrolled in such scholarship programs would attend institutions providing instruction primarily in English. RAND was asked to consider all aspects of the scholarship system, including its purpose, outcomes, policies, and procedures.

Three questions guided our inquiry:

1. What are the country's goals for its scholarship system, and what key principles underscore prestigious scholarship programs around the world?
2. What are the strengths and weaknesses of the existing scholarship programs, given these goals and principles?
3. How should the scholarship system be redesigned to meet the country's needs?

This report provides answers to these questions and outlines recommendations for the new scholarship system in Qatar. These recommendations were guided by the needs of the nation and designed to be consistent with changes under way in other areas of Qatar's education system.

In this report, we describe our main findings regarding the then-current scholarship program's strengths and weaknesses, comparing Qatar's system to those of other countries. We base policy and programmatic recommendations for a new scholarship system on a set of goals

[4] To get a sense of the magnitude of this investment relative to other investments in post-secondary education, this figure compares to approximately 8,500 students enrolled in the Academic Bridge Program, Qatar University, and institutions in Education City (Academic Bridge Program data and Qatar University, undated). For Qatari students, tuition at these programs and universities is paid for by the Qatari government. However, many of the 8,500 students are non-Qataris who pay tuition.

and guiding principles. Goals were derived from interviews with key stakeholders, and principles were determined by analyzing prestigious scholarship programs in other countries. These principles were then confirmed to be important to Qataris through our interview process.

The system proposed for Qatar is relevant for a broad range of developing countries seeking to develop a highly skilled population to promote economic and social development. In particular, the work is relevant for policymakers in other countries attempting to supplement their in-country higher-education options with those available on the international market.

Methods and Data

To review Qatar's scholarship program, we examined key internal documents, including the first scholarship law, written in 1976, as well as a 2003 proposal to update this legislation. We also collected descriptive quantitative data on Qatari scholarship recipients, conducted interviews with multiple stakeholders, and researched selected scholarship programs from other countries.

Most of our secondary data came from the Ministry of Education (for years 1998–1999, 1999–2000, and 2000–2001) and from the Ministry of Education Scholarship Office (for the number of scholarship graduates as of 2002). Qatar Petroleum also provided us with a list of its sponsored students studying in the United States. Information from these lists was entered into spreadsheets. These data allowed us to calculate scholarship-funded enrollments by level (undergraduate versus graduate), country of study, institution type (e.g., community college versus research university), and major.

We used the name of the institution to gauge the institutional quality of the colleges and universities attended by scholarship students. Specifically, we linked the rank score from *Barron's*[5] (for universities in the United States) and *The Guardian* (for universities in the United Kingdom) to the name of the post-secondary institution attended by each Qatari in the scholarship system attending college in either the United States or the United Kingdom.

During this study's six-month period, we conducted more than 50 interviews in person and by phone in Qatar, the United States, the United Kingdom, and Singapore (see Appendix D for more information about interviewees; Appendix C contains sample interview protocols). We developed a list of interviewees through discussions among our team members and with the SEC. We also worked closely with a scholarship alumnus who now directs an educational institute in Qatar. His overview of the system and experiences with it helped us further hone our interviewee list. In addition, as we conducted interviews, we became aware of the importance of other individuals and added them to our list. For example, we had not originally planned to interview cultural attachés until we learned of the importance of their role in the system. We also learned about a U.S.-based student-support provider during our interviews with a Doha-based scholarship sponsor. Hence, some interviewees were added over the course of the study. Table 1.1 lists each type of interviewee, along with the primary information solicited from each group.

---

[5] We selected *Barron's* instead of *U.S. News and World Report* so that we could classify institutions using the same categorization scheme (e.g., "most competitive," "highly competitive"). *U.S. News and World Report* does not rank all U.S. institutions according to such categories.

Table 1.1
Types of Interviewees and Key Information Solicited from Each Group

Interviewee Type	Number	Information Solicited
SEC members[a]	1	Ideal mission and objectives of scholarship system, alignment of current system with societal needs, recommendations for change Adequacy of current post-secondary options Benefits of studying abroad
Qatar Foundation officers	5	Ideal mission and objectives of scholarship system, alignment of current system with societal needs, recommendations for change Adequacy of current post-secondary options Benefits of studying abroad
Ministry of Education Scholarship Office leaders	5	Scholarship process Student and alumni experiences and employment information Ideal mission, objectives for system, recommendations for change
Planning Council officials	2	Process for determining workforce needs Adequacy of current post-secondary options Ideal mission and objectives of scholarship system, alignment of current system with societal needs, recommendations for change
Ministry of Civil Services Affairs and Housing officials	1	Skills needed by employers of post-secondary graduates Experience with scholarship system and sponsorship process Ideal mission and objectives of scholarship system, alignment of current system with societal needs, recommendations for change
Other ministry scholarship sponsors, including Qatar University	17	Experience with scholarship system and sponsorship process Ideal mission and objectives of scholarship system, alignment of current system to societal needs, recommendations for change Benefits of studying abroad
Qatari private-sector scholarship sponsors	6	Experience with scholarship system and sponsorship process Ideal mission and objectives of scholarship system, alignment of current system to societal needs, recommendations for change Benefits of studying abroad
Scholarship students and alumni	16	Experiences with scholarship system Student and alumni experiences Ideal mission, objectives of scholarship system, recommendations for change
College officials in Education City and at College of the North Atlantic	2	Experience with scholarship system Preparedness of students for college-level work Recommendations for change
Cultural attaché officials	2	Process for supporting students, liaising with Qatar Ministry of Education, employers, and foreign universities Adequacy of current post-secondary options Ideal mission, objectives of scholarship system, recommendations for change
U.S.-based student-support provider	1	Process for supporting students, liaising with Qatar Ministry of Education, employers, foreign universities Students' satisfaction with system Satisfaction with role in scholarship system
Scholarship program administrators in other countries	5	Mechanisms for aligning scholarship systems with workforce and other societal needs Process for selecting, supporting, and financing students Reflections on barriers and facilitators of a successful scholarship system

[a] The SEC also provided input during the project's cycle, particularly during the interim briefing.

Each team member read all of the interview notes. We discussed the notes in two phases. First, we discussed and sketched the main processes and procedures of the scholarship system to be sure that we fully understood how it worked. Then, we analyzed and synthesized all of our impressions of the system to generate lists of goals, objectives, strengths, and weaknesses. We continued to refer to the notes throughout the writing process.

We conducted a review of other scholarship programs, which we divided into three categories: (1) U.S.-based employer-sponsored programs, (2) programs in other countries, and (3) prestigious U.S. and UK programs. We devised these categories to capture a wide variety of features from diverse scholarship programs. Because the SEC expressed strong interest in ensuring that its scholarship system was supporting workforce needs, we wanted to capture features of employer-sponsored scholarship programs. We also wanted to ensure that we had information on how other countries capture and support workforce needs. Finally, we gathered information on prestigious U.S. and UK programs to capture characteristics of scholarships geared toward other outcomes, such as creating future leaders, to respond to the SEC's desire that its system be aligned with nonworkforce outcomes as well.

Full details on the programs reviewed and their characteristics can be found in Appendixes A and B. For the prestigious U.S. and UK programs, we chose those that are highly selective and have had a long history of operation. For the employer-sponsored programs, we chose to focus on large companies with highly selective programs, as well as on companies that resemble those in Qatar (e.g., oil companies). For other countries' scholarship programs, we chose small, high-income countries that are similar to Qatar to the extent that they do not have a well-developed domestic higher-education system but do have a growing economy that demands increasing numbers of skilled workers. We also selected countries in which a proportion of students attended highly selective post-secondary institutions, since this was a goal held by SEC members. Of all of the scholarship programs in other countries that we reviewed, Singapore sent the highest proportion of students to highly selective English-language post-secondary institutions. Moreover, Singapore and Qatar are similar in population, size, and wealth.

We visited Singapore to learn firsthand about its advanced state-run scholarship system and interviewed five sponsors of scholarship students in both the private and public sectors. Interview questions elicited information on their motives for sponsoring students, focusing in particular on how they have aligned their programs to workforce and other societal needs. We also gathered details on their policies (e.g., student and institutional eligibility for sponsorship) and processes (e.g., financing and contracting with students). Finally, we asked about the outcomes of their programs, how they evaluate them, and recent changes made in response to evaluations.

Limitations and Caveats

The SEC accepted our recommendations and established the new Higher Education Institute (HEI) in September 2004. This institute adopted the goals and principles suggested in this report, along with most of our recommendations on scholarship programs and organizational structure. We are grateful to have had the opportunity to conduct this study and to help launch what has become a prominent and important institute in Qatar.

The HEI has, since its founding, transformed our ideas and suggestions in establishing an institute that is well suited to serve the country's needs. Because RAND's research ended when the recommendations were made, this report does not discuss the new institute's operations. Nor does it compare in any detail our recommendations to the new organization. Instead, it summarizes our evaluation of the old system and the resulting recommendations. The success of these recommendations depends on how they are implemented.

There are several limitations to the generalizability of this study's recommendations. Perhaps chief among them is that Qatar is a country with generous resources for investment in its education system. Therefore, although our recommendations were designed to be efficient and cost was considered, these factors did not serve as prominent constraints.

It is also important to note that this study is about scholarships and is silent on Qatar's strategies for financing Qatar University, the College of the North Atlantic, and institutions in Education City. Although there is certainly overlap between financing a scholarship system and supporting post-secondary education in general, we do not address the latter, more general topic.

Finally, it is important to note that there have been other studies on Qatar's post-secondary system since we completed this one (see, especially, Stasz et al., 2007).

Organization of This Report

Chapter Two provides goals and guiding principles for a new scholarship system, based both on the results of our interviews and our analysis of other scholarship programs. Chapter Three explores the strengths and weaknesses of the scholarship programs as they existed at the time of this study. In Chapter Four, we present our recommendations for new scholarship programs. Chapter Five outlines an infrastructure for these new programs, as well as implementation guidance. We conclude in Chapter Six by explaining how the new system addresses each goal and underlying principle. We also briefly discuss how our recommendations connect to the current context of education reform in Qatar and the establishment of the HEI.

Appendix A provides details of employer-sponsored, government-sponsored, and prestigious scholarship programs that informed our proposal for Qatar's scholarship system. Appendix B provides information on scholarship programs in countries with similarities to Qatar, as well as findings from RAND's site visit to Singapore. Appendix C includes selected interview protocols used in our qualitative research, and Appendix D lists the numbers and affiliations of our interviewees.

CHAPTER TWO

Goals and Guiding Principles for Qatar's Scholarship System

When RAND was asked to conduct this study, members of the SEC stressed the importance of ensuring that the education system meet current demands for specialized human capital and prepares Qatari citizens to become future leaders. During the six-month study period, we asked these members and other stakeholders to elaborate on their goals for both the education system in general and a scholarship system in particular. This chapter presents a synthesis of the results of those interviews.

During our interviews, stakeholders conveyed that a new scholarship system for Qatar should be one that (1) motivates students in the primary- and secondary-education system; (2) encourages decisions about post-secondary study that benefit students, employers, and the state; (3) facilitates students' transition from the primary and secondary system to the post-secondary system; (4) motivates performance at the post-secondary level; and (5) ensures wise investments in human resources through close monitoring and evaluation.

In designing a model scholarship system with these features, it is useful to base policy and programmatic decisions on a clear set of goals and guiding principles. The following goals and principles were generated through an iterative process. Interview notes from leaders of the country's education system, scholarship sponsors (including several major employers), scholarship recipients, and scholarship program graduates were synthesized to generate recurring goals and guiding principles as set forth by the interviewees. We also outlined the goals and guiding principles of highly regarded scholarship programs worldwide. From these two efforts, we generated an initial list, which was presented to the SEC for feedback at an interim briefing.

Goals

We recommended that a new scholarship system work toward the following goals, based on our interviews and analyses of scholarship programs worldwide.

1. *Meet workforce needs.* In Qatar, there is a shortage of nationals with skills demanded by the labor market. Many interviewees stressed the importance of ensuring that scholarships support Qataris who are developing the skills deemed important by employers. At the time of this study, Qatari employers used scholarship programs as recruiting tools, a strategy employed in other countries as well. A scholarship system in Qatar should be both a recruiting tool and a mechanism for ensuring that students are developing skills that benefit the economy.

2. *Develop language, critical-thinking, and problem-solving skills.* Most scholarship graduates in Qatar are in demand because of their English-language skills. In addition, many students studying abroad believed that they were challenged to think more critically than they were while studying in Qatar. A scholarship system should support the development of high-level skills in language, as well as in critical thinking and problem solving, by encouraging study at high-quality post-secondary institutions.
3. *Prepare future leaders.* Many scholarship programs are used as vehicles for recruiting and preparing future leaders. Interviewees agreed that Qatar would benefit from a scholarship system that systematically selects and develops students for future leadership roles, in both the private and public sectors. We recommended that a scholarship system incorporate leadership training components, such as targeted internships and opportunities to shadow current government and business leaders in Qatar.
4. *Build cultural awareness of and ties to other countries.* Other countries we examined, including Singapore, use their scholarship programs to build international awareness and partnerships. Qatari employers stressed the importance of employees learning about foreign business systems and cultures. According to our interviews, Qatari students and scholarship alumni have benefited from their interactions with others abroad, both in terms of improving their language skills and in deepening their understanding of other cultures. High-quality post-secondary institutions are now available in Doha, and these could be given priority in a redesigned scholarship system. However, the option to study abroad should remain to ensure that employers and individuals reap the cultural and economic benefits that accrue from studying in a foreign country.
5. *Meet civic and cultural needs.* Interview respondents recommended that some of the best and the brightest Qatari students be allowed to pursue interests in fields that benefit society but may not directly benefit the economy, such as political science, art, music, and literature. In Singapore, employers allow students to choose almost any field of study, even if it does not directly relate to the scholarship student's future job. Although employers in Qatar have an overwhelming need for employees with specific skills, it is important to allow some flexibility, in order to develop human capital in an array of fields.

Guiding Principles

In structuring a scholarship system, it is important to align key decisions with these goals. It is also useful to anchor decisions in guiding principles, which address how the system should operate to achieve its goals. The following five guiding principles provided a foundation for our recommendations. They are key components of the highly regarded scholarship programs we studied, and interview respondents in Qatar confirmed the importance of these key principles.

1. *Quality.* Attending high-quality post-secondary institutions allows students to interact with motivated peers and learn from distinguished faculty members. A scholarship system should encourage attendance at the highest-quality institutions possible, given the recipient's qualifications.

2. *Accountability.* Recipients should be held accountable for their performance, with scholarship continuation dependent on achievement. Recipients need a sense of responsibility for the investment of public funds in their future.
3. *Efficiency.* A scholarship system should have streamlined procedures that include mechanisms for promptly addressing requests. Such procedures should capitalize on technology to reduce paperwork and increase the pace of decisionmaking. Clear policies and procedures that are available to all constituents would also help to improve efficiency through reducing or eliminating guesswork and idiosyncratic decisionmaking. Coordination across the entire scholarship system is also necessary to ensure efficiency.
4. *Flexibility.* Many Qatari scholarship recipients desired more flexibility in choosing (and revising choices of) countries and fields of study. A scholarship system could capitalize on this desire by rewarding top-performing recipients with greater flexibility.[1]
5. *Support.* Qatari students reported that they were poorly prepared for the challenges they faced in college. Students need adequate assistance in Qatar to make post-secondary decisions, such as choosing courses of study, institutions, countries, and scholarship options. Students who choose to study abroad should receive guidance before leaving Qatar to help ease their transition and should have access to coordinated support services during their period of study. In addition, students should receive information on employment options upon graduation.

---

[1] As will be explained in greater detail in Chapter Four, we recommended offering the most flexibility to top performers. This recommendation was based on client feedback regarding financial constraints guiding the design of the system, the need to ensure that students were studying at high-quality institutions and programs, and the desire to provide an incentive and reward for high achievement.

CHAPTER THREE

Qatar's Scholarship Programs

In this chapter, we outline features of Qatar's scholarship system at the time of our study, including data on the selectivity of institutions attended by scholarship recipients. In our attempt to determine the extent to which these features align with the goals and principles listed in Chapter Two, we analyze here some of the strengths and weaknesses of the system at the time of this study.

Description of the Scholarship System in 2003

The Qatari scholarship program was officially instituted through a law signed by the former Emir of Qatar in 1976. This 1976 law states that the purpose of the scholarship program is to allow students to "undertake academic, technical or practical study or obtain an academic qualification or acquire a practical skill in order to fulfill a shortage or a need mandated by public interest."

Scholarship programs in Qatar take on a variety of forms, depending on who administers and funds the program. At the time of this study, there were three main scholarship programs in the country: (1) Ministry of Education–sponsored program, (2) employer-sponsored programs, and (3) joint Ministry of Education– and employer-sponsored programs. Students applied for scholarships after secondary-school graduation for both undergraduate and graduate programs in many countries around the world. Figure 3.1 depicts the countries where Ministry of Education and Qatar Petroleum scholarship recipients were studying in 2002.

A 2003 proposal to amend the 1976 law was quite similar to the original legislation, albeit with stricter selection criteria and terms. The proposed law would have raised the GPA requirements for obtaining a scholarship and would have restricted the number of scholarship programs offered.[1] In addition, the scholarship committee proposed under the new law would have diminished the Ministry of Education's influence over its scholarship program by including more members from other ministries as part of the decisionmaking body.

Ministry of Education Program

As Table 3.1 shows, the Ministry of Education program supported close to 1,050 Qatari students on both external (i.e., abroad) and internal (i.e., in-country) scholarships in academic year 2000–2001, the most recent year for which data were available at the time of the study.

[1] Under the 1976 law, students not meeting the conditions for any of the "regular" scholarship programs could still be sponsored to go abroad for short-term training.

Figure 3.1
Countries of Study for Ministry of Education and Qatar Petroleum Scholarship Recipients, 2002

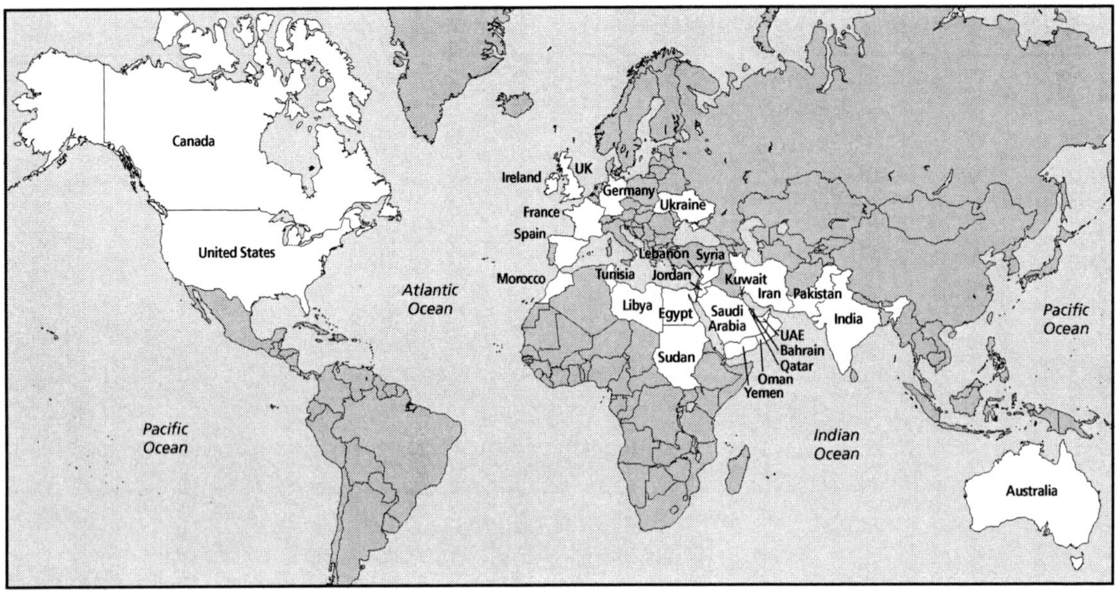

SOURCES: Qatar Ministry of Education data, 2000–2001, and Qatar Petroleum Corporate Training Department data, 2003.
RAND *TR478-3.1*

This includes not just students in their first year of scholarship-supported study but, rather, the cumulative total of all scholarship-supported students at that time. Almost 60 percent of the scholarship recipients were undergraduate students. At the time of this study, the Ministry of Education was sponsoring between 200 and 300 new scholarship recipients each year. On

Table 3.1
Distribution of Students with Ministry of Education Scholarships for Domestic and Foreign Study, 2000–2001

	Undergraduate Students		Graduate Students		Total Students			
Country	Number	%	Number	%	Number	%	Undergraduate Students, as % of Total	Graduate Students, as % of Total
Arab countries (including Qatar)	231	37	109	26	340	32		
United States	199	32	118	28	317	30		
United Kingdom	105	17	146	34	251	24		
Other Western countries	80	13	53	12	133	13		
Other	5	1	1	0	6	1		
Total	620	100	427	100	1,047	100	59	41

SOURCE: Qatar Ministry of Education data, 2000–2001.

NOTE: Numbers in table represent a snapshot of scholarship students in one year and include several cohorts of secondary-school graduates.

average, about 8 percent of Qatari high-school graduates in a given year received a Ministry of Education scholarship to begin their undergraduate studies.[2] About a third of all scholarship recipients studied in Arab countries (including Qatar), followed by 30 percent studying in the United States and 24 percent studying in the United Kingdom. Most recipients studied engineering, business, or health-related fields.[3]

The Ministry of Education scholarship program followed policies and procedures outlined in the 1976 law. The program was financed by the government of Qatar through the Ministry of Education and operated by the Ministry of Education Scholarship Office.[4] This office managed the application and selection processes and maintained contact with students to respond to requests and remediate problems that they encountered while abroad. The selection body, the Scholarship Committee, was composed of (up to) eight members, including Minister of Education officials and others appointed by the education minister, including the director of the Scholarship Office.

Contact with students and student support was handled through the Qatar cultural attaché's office in each of the countries where recipients studied. The office was also responsible for obtaining and disbursing monies to pay recipients' tuition and stipends. Recipients sent their transcripts and progress reports to the cultural attaché's office, which, in turn, reported back to the Ministry of Education Scholarship Office in Qatar. None of this was done electronically, and recipients reported that cultural attaché representatives were not always timely in their responses to student requests.

Every year, two or three weeks after the results of the high-school exit exam were published, the Ministry of Education Scholarship Office published a newspaper advertisement for students wishing to apply to study abroad or in Education City. This advertisement also included information on required Test of English as a Foreign Language (TOEFL) and high-school exit exam scores and a list of approved majors. The Ministry of Education was strict about what fields of study it was willing to sponsor. These fields were dictated by the country's labor needs in the short and medium term. The scholarship committee—with help from the Planning Council and using Qatar's five-year plans for economic development—decided which majors were needed most by the country and therefore eligible for scholarships.

In 2003, the approved majors were engineering (petroleum, chemical, electrical, mechanical, gas, security, architectural, water resource, medical, telecommunications, genetic, and industrial), flight systems, air transportation, interior design, medicine, dentistry, veterinary medicine, genetics, pharmacology, and statistics. There were no scholarships available for stu-

---

[2] The Ministry of Education does not collect information on the proportion of high-school graduates served by scholarships. The 8 percent figure should be considered a rough estimate and is calculated by using the number of undergraduate Qatari students on scholarship in a given year and linking this number to the number of graduating Qatari high-school students over the preceding four years. In addition, it should be noted that this is only the percent of Qatari high-school graduates who received a Ministry of Education scholarship at the undergraduate level. We were not able to collect the number of undergraduate students on scholarships from the other scholarship programs.

[3] We recognize that it would also be informative to provide breakdowns of students by gender and by masters and doctoral level within the graduate category. In addition, a critical factor to assessing a scholarship program is completion rates or years to degree. Unfortunately, these data were not available.

[4] We were not able to obtain cost data—annual expenditures, per-student expenditures, or total costs—for the existing Ministry of Education scholarship program or for the other two main scholarship programs operating at the time of this study, so they were not included in our analysis. We recognize that cost data on the existing programs are critical in assessing the relative benefits of the existing scholarship programs versus any proposed programs.

dents who wanted to study in other fields. These students could, however, attend Qatar University, which charges no tuition to Qataris.

The Ministry of Education supported scholarship students at nearly all types of post-secondary institutions, including some community colleges. Selection for a scholarship was not conditional on acceptance to a university. And in most cases, students received the scholarship before they were admitted into a post-secondary institution. Table 3.2 summarizes the key features of the Ministry of Education scholarship program.

Employer-Sponsored Programs

In addition to the Ministry of Education's scholarship program, students could obtain scholarships for undergraduate and graduate study through state-owned enterprises, such as Qatar Petroleum and Q-Tel. These scholarship programs were managed and financed by the individual companies,[5] which developed their own policies and procedures. Company policies were usually designed to meet the employer's labor needs. Students wishing to apply to an employer-sponsored program had to comply with eligibility and other requirements set forth by the employer.[6] Students received full tuition, a salary, travel allowances, and other benefits and were required to work for the employer upon graduation. Table 3.3 summarizes the key features of employer-sponsored programs.

Qatar Petroleum's scholarship program was the largest employer-sponsored program in Qatar. As Table 3.4 shows that, in 2003, its program supported close to 430 students on both external and internal scholarships. Externally, students tended to study in the United States and other Western countries, including Australia and France. Internal scholarships were

Table 3.2
Key Features of the Ministry of Education Scholarship Program

Requirement	Description
Application	Applicants respond to the Ministry of Education annual advertisement.
Selection criteria	Minimum TOEFL score of 500 is required for most majors (550 for engineering programs) if applying for study in an English-speaking country. Minimum 80th percentile on high-school exit exam is required for most majors (85th percentile for engineering; 90th percentile for medicine). Applicant must choose from the approved majors.
Award and obligations	Award covers full tuition, fees, stipend, and other allowances. Recipient must return to Qatar and work for a Qatari employer for double the time spent on scholarship-supported study.
Follow-up and support	Recipient follow-up and support are done through the cultural attaché's office in each country or region. Recipient information is not kept electronically.

SOURCE: Interview data.

[5] Given that these are state-owned enterprises, the state obviously assumes some financial responsibility, even though the programs are under the direction of and directly financed through the individual enterprises.

[6] For example, Qatar Petroleum required that applicants have a certain score on the high-school exit exam, a TOEFL score of at least 550, an SAT score of at least 450 on the verbal section and at least 450–550 on the math section (depending on whether the scholarship was for a technical or nontechnical degree program), and a certain score on an entry test (usually an Academic Bridge Program test) and pass a formal interview.

Table 3.3
Key Features of Employer-Sponsored Scholarship Programs

Requirement	Description
Application	Applicants apply to each employer directly.
Selection criteria	Minimum TOEFL score Minimum percentile on high-school exit exam Minimum SAT score Applicant must choose one of the approved majors.
Award and obligations	Full tuition, fees, stipend, and other allowances Employee salary Recipient must return to Qatar and work for employer for a specified period.
Follow-up and support	Recipient follow-up and support are done by the employer. Some employers subcontract support services to private companies in the countries where recipients are studying.

SOURCE: Interview data.

Table 3.4
Distribution of Students with Qatar Petroleum Scholarships, 2003

Country	Number of Students	%
Qatar (Qatar University and Texas A&M)	59	14
Other Arab countries (excluding Qatar)	26	6
United States	130	30
United Kingdom	47	11
Other Western countries (e.g., Australia, France)	167	39
Total	429	100

SOURCE: Qatar Petroleum Corporate Training Department data.

concentrated at Qatar University and Texas A&M in Education City.[7] All of Qatar Petroleum's scholarship students studied engineering.

Hybrid Programs

In addition to employer-sponsored and Ministry of Education scholarship programs, there was a third set of scholarship programs run by employers (in most cases, another ministry or government body) but subject to Ministry of Education rules and policies. (See Table 3.5 for key features of hybrid programs.) These programs were usually targeted to meet the labor-force needs of the sponsoring employer. The Ministry of Education funded these joint programs, but employers paid recipients' salaries. Because these programs followed Ministry of Education rules and policies, the application procedures, selection criteria, and award terms were the same as those for the Ministry of Education program. Recipients on hybrid scholarships were usually obligated to work for their employer-sponsor upon return to Qatar. An example of this type of program was the Ministry of Foreign Affairs program, which sponsored approximately

[7] Tuition at Qatar University and at institutions in Education City is free for Qataris. Students sponsored by an employer scholarship would receive a salary while studying at these universities.

Table 3.5
Key Features of Hybrid Scholarship Programs

Requirement	Description
Application	Applicants apply to each employer directly.
Selection criteria	Same selection criteria as Ministry of Education program Applicant must choose from employer-approved majors.
Award and obligations	Same award package as Ministry of Education program Employer-paid salary Recipient must return to Qatar and work for employer for a specified period.
Follow-up and support	Recipient follow-up and support are done by employer through the cultural attaché's office.

SOURCE: Interview data.

15 recipients at any given time at institutions inside Qatar (such as the College of the North Atlantic and VCU) and abroad. These recipients were sponsored in majors important to the Ministry of Foreign Affairs, such as languages, law, and graphic design.

Strengths and Weaknesses of the Current System

Strengths

Interviewees emphasized three main strengths of the scholarship system in Qatar:

- *Opportunity.* Scholarships provided undergraduate and graduate students the opportunity to go abroad to study in programs and for degrees not available in Qatar, which benefited both employers and recipients.
- *Generosity.* Recipients appreciated the financial support of the system. Awards were generous, and most students received enough funds to support them and their families while they studied full time in almost any country.
- *Cultural ties.* Many Qatari scholarship students studied abroad. Qatari employers emphasized that they benefited from the diversity of knowledge and skills that scholarship students gained in other countries. Scholarships exposed students to new ideas, work styles, and ways of life while building ties between Qatar and other countries.

Weaknesses

These advantages notwithstanding, the scholarship system in Qatar suffered from serious weaknesses. These weaknesses, determined through interviews and a review of highly regarded scholarship programs around the world, can be grouped in the following categories.

Policies and procedures were incomplete and inconsistently executed. We believe that the primary flaw of the scholarship system was the high level of problematic and inconsistent policies and actions. Because the scholarship law and program guidelines were rigid, they failed to address the range of possible student situations. Guidelines were therefore commonly modified on an ad hoc basis. This provided the system with some flexibility, but the cost was that recipients were virtually unable to navigate the process without the help of cultural attachés who, with good intentions, steered the recipients toward limited paths (often determined by a cultural attaché's personal connections or experience with a particular university). The highly idiosyncratic nature of the system ultimately had negative consequences in terms of the amount and quality of information available to recipients.

Recipients commonly used scholarships at low-ranking institutions. Many of the scholarship recipients sponsored by the Ministry of Education and other employers studied at low-ranked four-year institutions and community colleges. Figure 3.2 summarizes the types of institutions attended by graduates who received scholarships from the Ministry of Education for study in the United States and the United Kingdom in 2002. The categories (e.g., most competitive, noncompetitive) are those used by *Barron's* to rank U.S. post-secondary institutions and by *The Guardian* to rank UK post-secondary institutions. For example, according to *Barron's*, in general, colleges on the "most competitive" list require that students have a high-school rank in the top 10 percent to 20 percent and grade averages of A to B+. In addition, these colleges generally admit only a small percentage of those who apply—usually, fewer than one-third.

As shown in Figure 3.2, 6 percent of the recipients in the United States and 7 percent in the United Kingdom attended the most competitive institutions. Moreover, more than 40 percent of recipients in the United States and 60 percent in the United Kingdom attended universities classified as competitive, less competitive, or noncompetitive. Given the Qataris' desire to ensure that their investments in the scholarship program were being spent on highly selective institutions, these attendance patterns raised concerns as to the quality of education that scholarship recipients were obtaining.

The application and selection processes may have affected recipients' choices of less selective institutions. The application was poorly timed to encourage study at highly ranked colleges and universities. Students could not apply for scholarships until the summer after their senior

Figure 3.2
Rankings of Institutions Attended by Graduates of the Ministry of Education Program, 2002

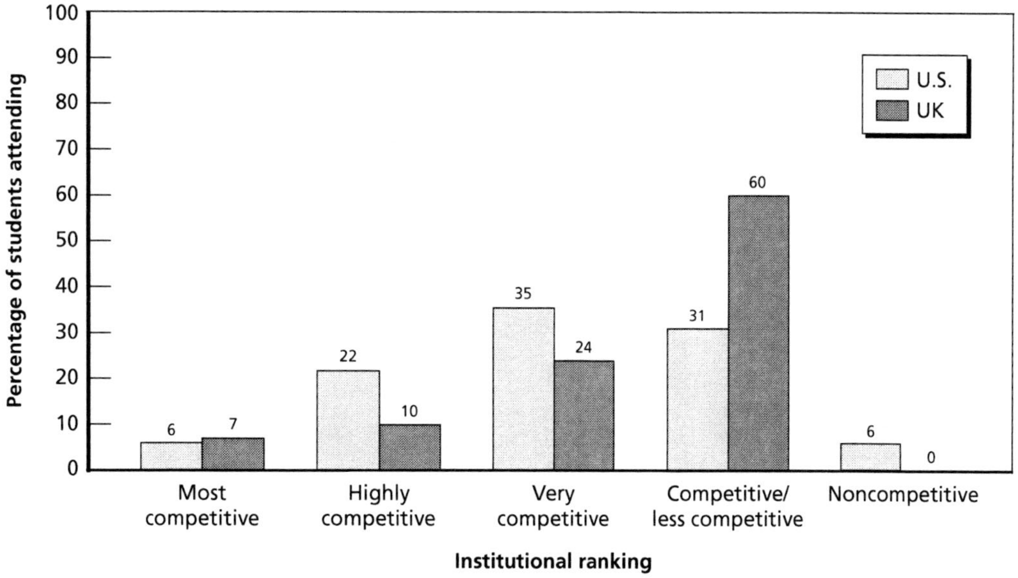

SOURCES: Graduate information from Ministry of Education Scholarship Office data. Rankings based on *Barron's Guide to the Most Competitive Colleges* (2001) and EducationGuardian (2003).

RAND *TR478-3.2*

year of high school, which came later than the application deadlines of many selective institutions in the United States and other parts of the world.[8]

Another factor that may have indirectly encouraged scholarship study at low-ranked institutions was the selection criteria for scholarships. Selection for scholarship awards was based largely on scores on the Qatari high-school exit exam, which has not been shown to be correlated with any measure of aptitude or post-secondary entrance requirements. For example, the Qatari high-school exit exam has not been calibrated to correlate with a high score on the TOEFL, SAT, or Graduate Record Examination (GRE), which most prestigious universities in the United States use to select candidates. Therefore, there is not necessarily a relationship between receiving a Qatari scholarship and the likelihood of admission to a high-quality university. In addition, because scholarships were given prior to students' acceptance to a university, students had little incentive to apply to selective institutions.

There were few incentives to study at highly selective institutions. While the scholarship law offered some incentives, these did not include incentives for students to seek academic rigor. Over the years of administering scholarships, incentives have included monetary bonuses for students in health-related disciplines (e.g., medicine, nursing, dentistry, veterinary medicine, pharmacology), marine-related disciplines, and petroleum or gas engineering. Recipients also received bonuses as a reward for achieving good grades at the end of the academic year. These field and grade incentives were for undergraduates only. Graduate recipients received a financial bonus if they graduated before the end of the period allocated for the study program.

While these incentives may have encouraged students to achieve good grades and, perhaps, to accelerate their studies, they did not encourage students to strive for admission to prestigious universities. Rather than motivating students to choose challenging post-secondary institutions, they may have done the opposite. During our interviews, recipients told us that they preferred to study at "easy" colleges in the United States—because they could more easily achieve good grades and possibly accelerate their studies and because employment and salaries were not tied to post-secondary institutional quality. All scholarship recipients had de facto guaranteed jobs upon return to Qatar, and they received the same salary and stipend regardless of institution attended or grades received.

Support services for recipients were inconsistently designed and delivered. At the time of our study, secondary students received no counseling or college preparatory services to ensure that they applied to the best institutions for their interests and abilities and Qatar's needs. Some students who were awarded a scholarship attended a Ministry of Education–sponsored orientation. However, those who participated reported that they received little guidance on adjusting to life in a new country.

Employer-sponsored recipients seemed to fare better in this regard. Qatar Petroleum, for example, subcontracted support services to a private company in Texas, where most of its scholarship recipients were studying. This company provided general guidance to recipients about studying abroad (e.g., life skills, such as how to get a driver's license; English classes; university registration assistance). However, the level of support given to recipients was uneven, with recipients in Texas obtaining more support than those studying in other states.

Support services and guidance for Ministry of Education and hybrid program scholarship recipients varied depending on the cultural attaché or adviser at the cultural attaché's office.

---

8 It is important to note, however, that many secondary-school graduates in Qatar would need additional study in English before meeting eligibility requirements at most selective institutions.

For example, some recipients had a "great" relationship with the cultural attaché's office and received adequate information and guidance. Others rarely had contact with the office and felt that they really needed guidance but did not know where to get it. Part of the problem was that recipients did not have easy access to former recipients who could share experiences and advise them, and the scholarship system did little to facilitate this kind of networking.

Applicants and recipients received insufficient information. The scholarship system did not provide adequate information to applicants or recipients. For example, despite the existence of very sophisticated information on post-secondary education around the world, the Ministry of Education provided recipients with limited, poorly produced, and out-of-date printed materials about universities and programs. Most recipients learned about universities and their programs through word of mouth or through the cultural attaché's office. Combined with a lack of counseling services at secondary schools, students had little up-to-date, objective information that they could use to make informed decisions.

In addition, no office within the system collected data in electronic or any other format that would allow for following up with scholarship recipients to determine the ultimate outcomes of scholarship-supported education. Therefore, it was difficult to know whether the various scholarship programs were fulfilling their mission of developing skills and filling labor shortages. Our research team encountered significant barriers to obtaining data about the system. Despite repeated requests, we were unable to obtain, either from the Ministry of Education or from Qatar Petroleum, an electronic list of students and their characteristics, contact information, institutions attended, and programs of study. Nor were we able to obtain budget figures for the Ministry of Education Scholarship Office to evaluate how they were using the resources available to them.

CHAPTER FOUR

Recommendations for New Scholarship System Programs

The system for awarding scholarships in Qatar was aligned neither to the goals that key stakeholders espoused for a scholarship system nor to the principles undergirding prestigious scholarship programs worldwide. Qatar needed a new scholarship system that considered scholarships as part of a broader education system and aimed to improve human capital and promote other social and cultural goals. To meet the diverse goals for a new scholarship system, we recommended three new scholarship programs: a prestigious scholarship program to support the education of a handful of exceptional students at the most competitive institutions around the world, an employer-sponsored program to meet the labor market demands of Qatar's employers, and a loan-based program that would add flexibility to the system by supporting students who are either not accepted or choose not to apply to either of the other programs.[1]

While distinct, the three programs would have common features that promote a systematic approach to awarding scholarships. All Qataris of any age who have completed secondary school would be eligible for one or more of the scholarship system's three programs. Non-Qataris could be eligible for the loan-based program.

Prospective applicants would be required to apply to universities prior to or concurrent with their application to scholarship programs, and scholarship awards would be contingent on university acceptance. Only applicants who have been accepted to an approved degree program and institution would receive a scholarship or loan.[2]

Scholarship and loan recipients would sign a contract that specifies student and sponsor obligations. While applicants could choose to be considered for more than one scholarship program, recipients would be allowed to participate in only one program. Students attending domestic and foreign institutions would be eligible for scholarship support. Qatari stakeholders stressed the importance of supporting domestic institutions in a new scholarship system in light of investments made in establishing high-quality branch campuses of foreign universities in Education City. Another consideration in the prioritization of domestic institutions was that some families do not allow their daughters to study abroad without a male relative in escort.

---

[1] We recognize that these three programs do not include a "merit" scholarship program for students who do not reach the level required to participate in the prestigious program and who are not ready to make a career employment decision. This is due, in part, to client feedback that the design of a model system should recognize financial constraints. In addition, the scholarship system should ensure that students attend high-quality institutions and programs. Further, the precollege grant program, addressed later in this chapter, is designed to prepare secondary students who may not be top performers to become eligible for high-quality institutions and scholarships.

[2] We considered the loan program as one of the scholarship programs, so information describing scholarships is also applicable to students receiving loans.

Moreover, scholarship recipients stressed that it has become increasingly difficult to obtain necessary student visas since the terrorist attacks in the United States on September 11, 2001.

Table 4.1 presents common features across scholarship programs and answers the following questions:

- Eligibility: Who would be eligible to participate in the three scholarship programs?
- Application: What would the application process entail?
- Selection: What would be the common selection criteria and how would recipients be selected?
- Awards and obligations: What would be the awards and obligations of all scholarship recipients?

Table 4.1
Proposed Common Features Across Scholarship Programs

Requirement	Description
Eligibility	All Qataris who have completed secondary school could apply for a scholarship or loan. Qataris of any age could apply. Undergraduate and graduate students could apply.
Application	Applicants must apply to universities prior to or concurrent with applications to scholarship programs. Applicants could apply to more than one scholarship program. Applicants propose level of study (i.e., undergraduate or graduate), field of study, and specific universities. All applicants submit the same application form, which includes a list of universities to which they applied, planned majors, student ID numbers, and demographic information. Applicants submit copies of their scholarship applications, university application forms, and personal essays. Given that applicants are applying to degree programs around the world with different deadlines, there would be multiple deadlines for submitting scholarship applications.
Selection	Only applicants who have been accepted into an approved degree program and institution receive a scholarship or loan. Recipients may be accepted to more than one scholarship program but may participate in only one program. All scholarship programs support study at Education City universities and at universities abroad. Applicants must be admitted to institutions at which the proposed program of study is of higher quality than the equivalent program at Qatar University. Applicants admitted to degree programs abroad that are also offered at Education City will receive scholarships to study abroad only if the proposed institutions are of higher quality than Qatar University and the applicants were denied admission to equivalent Education City institutions.
Award and obligations	Scholarship recipients sign contracts stating student and sponsor obligations. Contracts include time allowed for program completion and acceptable performance levels. Contracts specify award terms and incentives, which may include higher scholarship stipends or lower loan interest rates for students who achieve high grades or finish programs before the allotted time. Contracts specify recipients' postgraduation obligations.

Unique Features of Proposed Scholarship System Programs

In addition to these common features, each scholarship program would have unique features designed to meet individual recipient needs and to contribute to achieving the economic, civic, and cultural needs of Qatar. One of the main differences across programs relates to eligibility. Only Qatari citizens would be eligible for the prestigious scholarship program, while non-Qataris could be eligible for the employer-sponsored program, as determined by individual employers. Non-Qataris could be eligible for the loan-based program as well. Another key difference is that the prestigious and loan-based programs would provide broader choices in terms of programs of study than would the employer-sponsored program. Finally, award packages and postgraduation employment requirements differ across programs. Tables 4.2, 4.3, and 4.4 present more detail on the unique features of each proposed program.

Prestigious Scholarship Program

The prestigious program is designed for the highest achievers, and receiving this type of scholarship would be considered a great honor. Recipients would have relatively broad choices in terms of program and level of study, as well as flexibility during their course of study and after graduation. Students studying as prestigious scholars could be provided with additional programs, such as leadership seminars and opportunities to network or intern with the country's leaders, to prepare these students to assume leadership positions in the future.

Table 4.3 presents the unique features of the prestigious scholarship program.

Recipients would have specific obligations during their course of study, as specified in their contracts. Continuation of the scholarship would be contingent upon maintenance of a C average or equivalent for undergraduate students and a B average or equivalent for graduate

Table 4.2
Proposed Unique Features Across Scholarship Programs

	Program		
Requirement	**Prestigious**	**Employer-Sponsored**	**Loan-Based**
Eligibility	All Qataris of any age who have completed secondary school could apply.	All Qataris of any age who have completed secondary school could apply. Sponsorship of non-Qataris determined by employers	All Qataris of any age who have completed secondary school could apply. Non-Qataris eligible under different loan terms
Application	Applicants have broad choice of program and level of study	Eligible programs and level of study based on employer needs	Applicants have broad choices of program and level of study.
Selection	Scholarship awarded automatically once applicant is admitted to highly selective, eligible university	Award contingent on admission to high-quality university Employers may select students.	Award contingent on admission to high-quality university
Award and obligations	Generous award package Relatively flexible postgraduation employment requirement	Award package set by employer Postgraduation employment requirement set by employer	Some students eligible for subsidized loans Recipient begins loan repayment upon graduation, unless employer pays on recipient's behalf. No postgraduation employment requirement

Table 4.3
Proposed Unique Features of a Prestigious Scholarship Program

Requirement	Description
Application	Applicants propose any program and level of study (undergraduate or graduate, including Ph.D.)
Selection	Prestigious scholarships awarded automatically once an applicant is admitted to a highly selective, eligible degree program or university, which may include Education City universities Top 50 U.S. degree programs and/or universities Top 10 UK degree programs and/or universities Top degree programs and/or universities in other countries.[a]
Award and obligations	Recipient award package to include full tuition and fees, generous monthly stipend (varying with country of study), annual book and computer allowance, travel allowance, health insurance, spousal and dependent stipend and air travel Awards, other than tuition and fees, identical for undergraduate and graduate students Recipients encouraged to study or to accept an internship during the summer months, and they continue to receive scholarship award for those months if they do so Recipients may change majors or universities with approval. Recipients have choice of employment upon completion of their degrees, but must work for a Qatar employer for the number of years spent on scholarship, an obligation that could be fulfilled any time within 10 years of graduation.

[a] The cutoffs for highly selective programs and institutions are based on SEC feedback at the interim briefing. These cutoffs should be seen only as guidelines; formal cutoffs would be based on the research and policy decisions of the administrators of the new system.

students in the program of study. (The required average may be higher if set by the university.) If a recipient does not maintain this minimal level of performance or drops out of the course of study, the scholarship would be revoked, but the student would not be obligated to repay monies spent.

In addition, the time allowed for study would be stipulated in each recipient's contract. Recipients would have the average length of time to finish their degree (e.g., four years for an undergraduate degree in the United States). Recipients could apply for a one-year extension. Guidelines for approval of extensions could include student demonstration of both a high level of academic achievement and the ability to complete the program in one additional year.

Employer-Sponsored Scholarship Program

The employer-sponsored program was designed to fill individual employer's labor-market needs. Therefore, recipients would have a limited choice of programs and levels of study. Table 4.4 presents the unique features of the employer-sponsored program.

All employer-sponsored scholarship programs in the country could be centrally administered. All government employers (e.g., ministries, Qatar University) in Qatar would offer scholarships through the central system, while state-owned enterprises (e.g., Qatar Petroleum) and private employers would be strongly encouraged to do so. Employers would retain autonomy over decisions related to scholarship terms, such as eligible courses of study, funding allowances, performance criteria, and repayment requirements, and would assume all costs related to recipient awards.

In exchange for opting in to the new system, employers could capitalize on a full range of services, including marketing, recruiting, student advising and selection, and student

Table 4.4
Proposed Unique Features of Employer-Sponsored Scholarship Program

Requirement	Description
Eligibility	Employers decide whether to sponsor students (Qatari or non-Qatari).
Application	Applicants must propose a program and a level of study (undergraduate or graduate, including Ph.D.) that are consistent with employer's needs.
Selection	Employers may elect to select recipients or may delegate this responsibility to the scholarship system administrators.
Award and Obligations	Award is employer-paid and so may vary from employer to employer. In general, award includes full tuition and fees, monthly stipend (varies by country of study), annual book and computer allowance, travel allowance, and health insurance. Award may include support for summer study or internship and spousal and dependent benefits, as determined by employer. Changes in majors or institutions of study must be approved. Recipients have specified years of employment obligation to employer sponsor immediately following graduation; recipient may be able to repay the employer scholarship monies rather than serve the work obligation.

orientation and support. These services would be available to employers at no cost, providing a strong incentive for them to opt in to the system. Employers who opt in would accept all of the general common guidelines described in Table 4.1 regarding application procedures, selection process, eligible institutions of study, and monitoring procedures.

In addition, employers would be expected to (1) specify majors and numbers of students needed for undergraduate and graduate levels of study, (2) draft and maintain contracts with students (concerning, e.g., funding allowances, performance criteria, payback requirements, length of study), (3) determine postgraduation employment requirements, and (4) pay all scholarship costs (e.g., tuition and fees, air travel, stipend). While the specific recipient obligations regarding performance, length of study, and repayment for noncompletion are to be set by each individual employer, the contracts would be administered and monitored by a central body. Employers would have final approval of recipient changes in programs or institutions of study.

This proposed program differs from the preexisting employer-sponsored scholarship program in several ways. Under the new system, employers would be relieved of many key duties, including selecting high-quality institutions and advising, supporting, and monitoring students. Employers would also benefit from a centralized tracking system that would monitor student outcomes by country, institution, and program of study to inform future scholarship decisions. The system as a whole, and scholarship recipients specifically, would benefit from a coordinated effort with clear policies, streamlined procedures, and universal support services prior to and during the period of study. Employers who opt in to this new system would relinquish the right to select colleges and universities, however. Hopefully, employers would want to send future employees to qualified programs. It would be important to work with employers to ensure that there are several qualified programs for all of their areas of need.

Loan-Based Scholarship Program

The third program within the proposed scholarship system was designed to allow students to take out loans to fund their higher-education studies. The loan-based program would offer an alternative to students who have not been accepted into the prestigious program or the employer-sponsored program or who want broad choice and flexibility over their course of study and postgraduation employment. The loan option adds flexibility to the scholarship system while ensuring recipient responsibility. Table 4.5 presents some of the unique features of the loan-based scholarship program.

Loan-based scholarship recipients would have specific obligations during their course of study, as specified in their contracts. Similar to the prestigious program, continuation of the loan would be contingent upon maintaining a C average or equivalent for undergraduate students and a B average or equivalent for graduate students in the program of study. (The required average may be higher if set by the university.) If a recipient does not maintain this minimal level of performance or drops out of college, the loan would be revoked, and the recipient would have to repay monies already disbursed. The time allowed for study would be stipulated in each recipient's contract. Recipients would have the average length of time to finish their degrees (e.g., four years for an undergraduate degree in the United States) but could apply for one-year extensions as under the prestigious scholarship program.

Precollege Grants

An ideal scenario for secondary-school students in the proposed system would be that they have the language skills and academic preparation to be accepted to high-quality institutions and receive scholarships upon graduation. To reach this goal, they would be encouraged to begin language training before they graduate from secondary school. However, some prospective scholarship applicants (undergraduate and graduate), particularly in the early years of the new system, will likely require additional language or academic preparation. In this proposed new system, these prospective applicants would be able to apply for a one-year precollege grant.

Table 4.5
Proposed Unique Features of a Loan-Based Scholarship Program

Requirement	Description
Eligibility	All Qataris and non-Qataris of any age who have completed secondary school
Application	Applicants can propose the program and level of study (undergraduate or graduate, including Ph.D.).
Selection	Loan-based scholarships will be awarded contingent on an applicant's acceptance to a high-quality university.
Award and obligations	A maximum loan amount includes full tuition and fees, monthly stipend, and other allowances up to the maximum amount given to students under the prestigious scholarship program. Loans granted for study during academic year or summer or for summer internship during summer break Recipients are not entitled to additional loans to support a spouse or dependents Maximum awards are identical for undergraduate and graduate recipients Qataris are eligible for subsidized loans, and loan terms may vary based on chosen field of study, university, and country of study. Loans to non-Qataris subject to market interest rates Recipients may change majors or universities with notification and approval. Recipients have no postgraduation employment requirement. Recipients begin loan repayments following completion of their course of study. An employer may choose to repay the loan for the recipient upon hiring the recipient.

NOTE: Institutions eligible for inclusion under the loan-based program would be determined by the proposed institutional standards office, as outlined in Chapter Five.

Receipt of precollege grants would be contingent on one or more of the following criteria: the applicant's secondary-school performance, language and other aptitude test results, the applicant's goals, and letters of recommendation. Precollege grant applicants would apply for the program that best meets their needs. Grants would be allocated for study at domestic programs, such as the Academic Bridge Program. Students could also apply to foundation or language programs abroad. Because Qatar supports multiple precollege preparation programs, preference would be given to applicants who choose a domestic option. To enforce this preference, grant awards would cover the cost of tuition only; they would not cover travel or living allowances. Recipients could request a second year of funding, which would be awarded on a case-by-case basis.

Study-Abroad Programs

Because we recommended the prioritization of domestic universities and more stringent criteria for scholarship awards, it is possible that the number of Qataris completing degree programs abroad will decline. Given that international exposure is an important goal of this proposed system, we recommended additional programmatic options to build cultural awareness of and ties to other countries. International exposure could be accomplished by increasing the number of students studying abroad for a short period, such as a semester. Students would apply for grants to cover their tuition and living allowances while studying abroad.

CHAPTER FIVE

Scholarship System Infrastructure and Implementation

This chapter recommends an organizational infrastructure for the new system and provides guidance on implementing it. Implementing the new programs described in Chapter Four would require significant physical and technological infrastructure changes. New organizations, staffed with world-class professionals, would be important components of the proposed system. Without the appropriate organizational structure and related staff, a scholarship system could not accomplish the key functions of ensuring adherence to common guidelines, designing incentives, tracking and evaluating performance, and providing extensive post-secondary advisement.

A New Post-Secondary Education Institute

Because post-secondary education in Qatar is undergoing significant changes, we recommended that a new organizational structure be implemented to manage the scholarship programs and also take on responsibility for overseeing post-secondary education more broadly, with a mission exceeding that of simply managing scholarship programs. Given the rapid pace of change in Qatar's post-secondary landscape, the result of both internal reforms and the recent arrival of several foreign branch campuses, it is important to coordinate, plan for, and monitor the quality of post-secondary education Qataris receive at home as well as abroad. This work would include evaluating in-country institutions, ensuring sufficient options for post-secondary study, and providing authorization and licensing for new colleges to operate in Doha. Much of this work is already done by the Qatar Foundation, and careful consideration would be needed to ascertain how to consolidate and coordinate all post-secondary duties—including essential post-secondary oversight and quality-assurance functions, as well as scholarship program functions.

Our research of other scholarship systems, as well as our stakeholder interviews, led us to conclude that a centralized body would be needed to ensure that the proposed scholarship system achieves its full potential. At the time of this study, the Ministry of Education coordinated the then-current scholarship system. Due to staffing limitations and structural impediments, it did not appear that the Ministry of Education had the capacity to spearhead a new scholarship system. Given the importance of ensuring adequate support and the lack of alternative options, we recommended establishing a new post-secondary education institute, both to administer the scholarships and execute other higher-education functions, such as authorization and accreditation.

The SEC would have authority over the new Post-Secondary Education Institute (PEI). The PEI, in collaboration with the SEC, would set vision and direction for policies and research related to post-secondary education in Qatar. At the time of this study, the SEC had legal responsibilities for all post-secondary education in the country. We therefore recommended that the SEC ensure coordination among policies and functions at Qatar University, the College of the North Atlantic, Education City, and the new PEI. We also recommended that the SEC evaluate the PEI through the research office in its Evaluation Institute.

The new PEI would house an institutional standards office, a scholarship office, and a student resource center. Each of these three offices would provide different functions to support all scholarship programs in the scholarship system (including the prestigious scholarship program, the employer-sponsored scholarship program, and the loan-based scholarship program). Figure 5.1 depicts the organizational structure for the proposed institute. We recommended combining foreign and regional expertise in staffing the institute, as well as retaining expert contractors for some of the work.

The Institutional Standards Office

We recommended that the institutional standards office conduct three primary tasks: determine institutional eligibility, conduct quality assurance for in-country post-secondary institutions, and execute research on higher-education topics.

An important component of the proposed scholarship system is to provide incentives for students to study in the highest-quality degree programs around the world. We recommended that, to study outside of Qatar, scholarship recipients be admitted to a degree program that is of higher quality than those offered at Qatar University.[1] This guideline was intended to help to ensure that the Qatari government was investing in scholarships to high-quality post-secondary institutions. To evaluate educational quality, the institutional standards office would employ expert researchers to consider established quality measures (e.g., program rankings) to

Figure 5.1
Proposed Organizational Structure for the Post-Secondary Education Institute and Its Offices

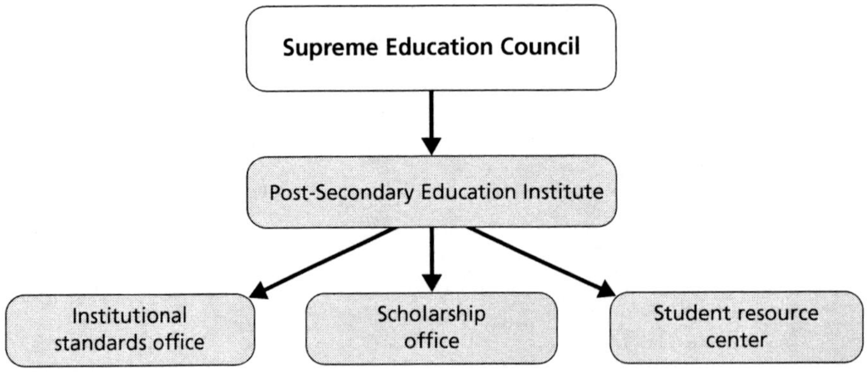

RAND *TR478-5.1*

[1] This does not suggest that students can study only for degrees offered at Qatar University. Scholarship students could study other degrees as long as they study at institutions that are of higher quality than Qatar University, as determined by the institutional standards office.

assess the quality of institutions around the world and compare them to Qatar University. Because there are no rankings of universities in the Middle East, it is difficult to position Qatar University against ranking lists from other countries. However, researchers in this office could consider the variables used in ranking systems and attempt to ascertain where Qatar University would be ranked on these lists. This process would be fairly complex and would involve gathering variables on Qatar University that are commonly used in other ranking systems, such as student-to-faculty ratios and numbers of peer-reviewed journal articles published by faculty members. Some ranking indicators may not be relevant, such as the quantity of alumni donations. Not only would these variables need to be collected on Qatar University, they would also be needed for other universities in the Middle East that are not currently ranked. This task would, admittedly, be very difficult and could take years to hone. We recommended starting with institutions commonly attended by Qataris under the old scholarship system, then ranking others gradually. It may also be wise to group institutions in broad categories, rather than determining a specific rank order.

Because post-secondary education in Qatar is undergoing significant changes, we recommended that this office in the PEI also apply quality-assurance mechanisms for foreign colleges and universities operating in the country. This work may include ensuring that Qatari stakeholders are well served by these institutions and that the colleges and universities are participating in their own countries' accreditation processes. Finally, we recommended that this office authorize and license new colleges to operate in Doha.

This office would also oversee all research design and analysis associated with the PEI, including establishing a post-secondary-education data system that is integrated with the Qatar National Education Data System (QNEDS). Using data on student performance and outcomes, staff would produce analytical reports on such topics as college choice, student performance, career choice, and job placement.

The Scholarship Office

This study concluded that, in the then-current scholarship system, policies and procedures were inconsistently designed and executed, support services for students were only sporadically provided, misaligned incentives were guiding choices, and information throughout the system was lacking. We recommended establishing a scholarship office to remedy these deficiencies.

This office would be the policymaking, administrative, and oversight body for all issues related to scholarships in Qatar, administering both government- and employer-sponsored scholarship programs. The office would introduce an efficient, merit-based, transparent process for allocating scholarships. Office staff would be committed to cultivating relationships with scholarship recipients, providing recipients with counseling and support during their studies, holding recipients accountable for contract terms, and providing career counseling and support after recipients complete their studies.

Members of this office would draft policies and procedures for the system, as well as program guidelines and incentive structures. The centralized guidelines would include scholarship eligibility criteria, precollege education options, and eligible countries, institutions, programs, and fields of study, including distance-learning programs. Office staff would also determine application deadlines, design forms, and administer the scholarship application process, including the screening and selection of applicants. Given that scholarship awards would be dependent on admission to an eligible university or college, there would not be extensive decisionmaking involved in granting scholarships.

The scholarship office would also coordinate employer-sponsored scholarships. In so doing, this office would consult with employers on a semiannual basis to assess national labor-market needs. These needs would guide office staff in determining which employers to target for sponsoring students on scholarships. Office staff would then work closely with sponsoring employers to design contracts and financial packages stipulating recipients' and sponsors' obligations. We recommended that all government employers (e.g., ministries) offer scholarships through the PEI, and all other employers in Qatar (e.g., those in the private sector) would be encouraged and invited by the SEC to do so. The PEI would be responsible for administering all aspects of the employer scholarships, adhering to guidelines as laid out by individual employers. Employers offering scholarships through the PEI would assume all costs related to recipient benefits (e.g., tuition, fees, air travel, stipend, salary) but would not be charged any administrative costs for services provided by the PEI, including marketing, recruiting, advising, selecting students, enacting financial transactions, and monitoring and supporting students. Staff would work with employers on selecting students, with employers having final approval of students, majors, and institutions.

Staff in this office would support students before, during, and after their study period. Providing support would include reviewing scholarship contract terms and obligations with recipients, assisting with visa applications and processing, hosting orientation events, interacting with international student offices at universities overseas, and establishing lines of communication among recipients and alumni. Staff would also ensure tuition and stipend payments, advise loan recipients, and manage all bank relations. After students graduate, staff would provide career guidance, link recipients with employers, and host networking events for alumni from different cohorts.

Finally, this office would be responsible for all issues related to tracking students and ensuring accountability. Staff would conduct extensive data collection to monitor recipients' progress, performance, and adherence to scholarship obligations and review any requests for changes in the contract, such as for transfers and extensions. Continuation of the scholarship or loan would depend on student performance, which we recommended as a C average or equivalent for undergraduate students and a B average or equivalent for graduate students throughout the course of study. Scholarship recipients would submit year-end transcripts to the scholarship office. The office would review the list of students who did not meet minimum performance levels, and scholarships or loans would be revoked under the terms set out in their contracts.

Student Resource Center

Under the old system, scholarship recipients received little guidance or direction about options available worldwide, and many recipients attended low-ranked academic institutions. Secondary-school students received little guidance or counseling about careers and post-secondary study. College and degree program choices were not guided by knowledge of career or academic options. This lack of information denied scholarship recipients and all residents interested in post-secondary education the opportunity to have the highest-quality academic experience possible. The RAND team recommended establishing a student resource center to introduce more information and options to Qatari residents motivated to study beyond secondary school.

The student resource center would serve as an information and counseling center for all Qatari residents interested in post-secondary education. We recommended that the center include a selective collection of databases related to career choice, undergraduate and graduate study, language training, "bridge" coursework, standardized-test preparation, and continuing education in various disciplines.

Center clients would have access to these databases and to advisers who would guide them through the college and degree program selection process. Staff would have current information on career opportunities in Qatar and would conduct outreach to secondary schools in need of career and post-secondary education counseling. Staff members could work with schools without guidance counselors, developing ongoing adviser relationships with individual students at these schools.

In addition to assisting all residents interested in post-secondary education, the student resource center would serve a number of other functions. Office staff would be responsible for hosting a scholarship fair and a university fair, sponsoring scholarship award ceremonies, disseminating annual reports, supervising the marketing of scholarships and services, and interacting with public officials and media. Once the center is operating at full capacity, its staff could assume the scholarship-related work now done by the cultural attachés. Alternatively, the cultural attachés could maintain their roles but receive better guidance and information from the center.

Implementation

The success of any reform design depends on its implementation. We recommended that an implementation team oversee this step, making key decisions about where, how, and when over the course of implementation. An ideal implementation team would be comprised of both foreign and Qatari experts. Implementing a new scholarship system requires both individuals with post-secondary education expertise who can evaluate options and make educated decisions and individuals with local knowledge who can ensure that these decisions align with the cultural and political context.

Similarly, we envisioned that the work of the PEI would be done by a combination of Qataris, a world-class professional staff, and short-term expert contractors. For example, a contractor might be best positioned to establish the student resource center. However, there could be a plan to transition management of this center to a Qatari manager in time.

The reconfigured scholarship system would entail considerable initial investment, because key components of the system require development. These include formal guidelines; policies and procedures related to student applications and acceptance, eligible countries, universities, and programs of study; and award amounts and loan terms. In addition, the successful implementation of the system would require the development of appropriate counseling services and college preparatory services for all residents, as well as systematic support for scholarship recipients during their course of study and postgraduation. The benefits of the counseling and other support services would potentially go beyond the scholarship system and affect the whole educational system.

Estimating the exact costs of implementing the proposed scholarship system is difficult due to a number of unknown factors. Costs depend on many variables, including the salaries needed to attract the best candidates, the distribution of functions contracted out and handled internally, the mix of resident and nonresident staff, the mix of junior and senior staff, and the extent to which employers opt in to services offered. Some start-up expenditures, such as for setting up the data system, developing the Web site, and establishing the scholarship guidelines, would occur, to a large extent, only one time. Although these tasks involve ongoing refinement, the major expenditures would be incurred up front as an initial investment.

CHAPTER SIX

Conclusion

In this chapter, we specify how the proposed system could meet Qatar's goals for its scholarship programs. We also describe how the principles identified in other high-quality scholarship programs relate to our recommendations. In assessing the proposed scholarship system's ability to meet the specified goals and guiding principles, it is important to recognize that the system will not operate in isolation. One must consider Qatar's related employment and labor policies, as well as social customs, that will interact with the reforms. In some cases, as discussed later in this chapter, these policies and customs may impede the full realization of the goals and guiding principles in practice. We conclude with a note about how these recommendations align with the broader educational reforms in Qatar and why they might be of interest to policymakers in other countries.

Proposed Scholarship System

Key Goals

Goal 1: Meet workforce needs. The proposed system would provide extensive precollege guidance to introduce information and options to all Qatari residents motivated to study beyond secondary school. This guidance would be backed by comprehensive research on institutional quality and Qatar's labor-market needs. Students could select high-quality institutions and programs of study to match their abilities and interests as well as the country's needs. The proposed system includes incentives for students to study in needed majors and degree programs and attend high-ranking institutions. The proposed infrastructure is designed to allow policymakers to offer additional incentives to complete degree programs within a reasonable period and excel in college. The system would facilitate the transformation of secondary-school students to highly skilled professionals. While all three scholarship programs in the proposed new system meet workforce needs, the employer-sponsored program, in particular, should directly meet Qatar's labor-market needs by directing students to specific fields of study.

Meeting this goal, however, requires that Qatari employers are able to project labor-market needs and that Qataris pursue in-demand occupations. Given that Qatar's economy is based on energy production, state-owned enterprises (such as Qatar Petroleum) and private-sector employers are likely able to project labor-market needs and make the right choices as to skill needs. This is less certain for the government sector, which has an implicit social contract that guarantees jobs for Qatari nationals and employs about 77 percent of the Qatari-national workforce. Further, a recent RAND study on post-secondary education in Qatar suggests that, while Qatar has ample opportunities for students to study in-demand occupations, Qataris do not necessarily make the "right" choices. The guarantee of government-sector jobs for Qatari nationals limit student incentives to pursue in-demand occupations. And, women, who are more highly educated than men, are not always able to freely choose career paths. Not all high-demand jobs are open to women, and women tend to choose from a narrow set of occupations (Stasz et al., 2007). Current employment policies and social customs in Qatar may therefore limit the full realization of this goal.

Goal 2: Develop language, critical-thinking, and problem-solving skills. The proposed system would establish methods to help Qatari students gain skills in each of these areas. First, by enabling selected students to pursue degree programs and short-term study abroad, it would allow those students to become immersed in other languages and cultures. Second, by promoting attendance at highly competitive institutions in Qatar and around the world, the system would place students in rigorous educational settings that engage them in critical thinking and problem solving. Third, the system would prepare students embarking on post-secondary study by providing funds for preliminary study in language and other subject areas before entering the degree program. Those students who study at Qatar University will also most likely be enrolled in programs in English, as the university is in the process of implementing its policy of English as the primary language of instruction.

Goal 3: Prepare future leaders. To prepare future leaders, Qatar must challenge its youth to excel academically, personally, and professionally and instill leadership qualities in students, such as discipline and motivation. By requiring that scholarship applicants seek education at the world's best colleges and universities, the system would encourage secondary students to excel academically to qualify for both scholarship awards and admission to highly selective colleges and universities. Scholarship recipients would study at rigorous institutions where they would be trained in the critical-thinking skills inherent in a high-quality education. After graduation, they would fulfill the duty of bringing their knowledge, critical-thinking skills, and leadership back to Qatar.

While the scholarship programs should instill key traits, such as discipline and motivation, they will also be important in directly imparting leadership skills by providing recipients with supplemental leadership training and opportunities to exercise leadership skills and interact with current leaders through internships and other training programs.

It is important to note that the successful realization of this goal assumes that students are motivated to excel and are encouraged by the incentives of studying at some of the best universities in the world and of broad-ranging employment opportunities upon program completion. In reality, the availability of virtually guaranteed, secure, and well-paying government jobs poses a disincentive for students to choose academically challenging paths (Stasz et al., 2007). While the proposed scholarship system will motivate some students, other employment policies in Qatar could limit the full realization of this goal.

Goal 4: Provide international exposure and establish ties to other countries. The proposed system would provide many students with the opportunity to study abroad, either in degree programs or in short-term study-abroad programs. The quality of the study-abroad experience would be improved by the fact that students would be required to attend selective universities and that students would receive information on and support to apply to study-abroad programs. Over time, the continuous flow of Qatari students to top universities worldwide would establish lasting connections among fellow alumni from around the world and between Qatar and prestigious institutions in other countries. Students who do not meet the qualifications to study abroad would be provided with opportunities for semesters and other short-term periods abroad.

Goal 5: Meet civic and cultural needs. The proposed system would allow students in two of the three scholarship programs to pursue interests in fields that may not directly benefit the economy, such as political science, art, music, and literature. While the employer-sponsored program would meet the need for employees with specific skills, the prestigious and loan-based programs would allow students flexibility to develop human capital in an array of fields that benefit Qatari society.

Guiding Principles

Our recommendations are guided by principles of quality, accountability, efficiency, flexibility, and support. These principles are common across the prestigious and country-based scholarship programs we reviewed and were endorsed by key Qatari stakeholders. In this section, we address how the proposed system would meet each of these guiding principles.

Quality. The proposed scholarship system would encourage attendance at the highest-quality institutions possible, given the students' qualifications. A scholarship recipient would need to be admitted to an institution at which the planned program of study is of higher quality than the equivalent program at Qatar University. Scholarship recipients would also be offered incentives for achieving outstanding grades and finishing their programs before the allotted time. These incentives are designed to motivate students to excel academically. Qatar's leadership will need to assess what types of incentives will do the most to encourage both attendance at high-quality institutions and academic excellence within the context of current employment and labor policies.

Accountability. The proposed system addresses accountability for both students and the system as a whole. Regarding students, scholarship recipients under the proposed system would be held accountable for their performance in three ways. First, recipients would sign contracts that specify student and sponsor obligations, including time allocated for program completion, acceptable performance levels, and postgraduation obligations. Second, continuation of the scholarship would be dependent on a certain level of achievement to ensure that scholarship monies are disbursed only to those who continue to perform well in their studies. Third, recipient performance would be tracked to ensure that students continue to meet their contract obligations.

The scholarship system would be accountable to students in a number of ways. First, the recipient contracts would specify government and employer responsibilities in addition to recipient responsibilities. Further, the merit-based, transparent process for allocating scholarships would ensure that students face consistent policies and actions rather than guidelines modified on an ad hoc basis. Concerning accountability of the educational system, we proposed data collection and analysis at the post-secondary level to track students from the time of their scholarship application through their post-secondary careers. These post-secondary data should be linked with the K–12 data system in QNEDS to allow evaluation of the whole educational system.

Efficiency. The proposed scholarship system would include streamlined procedures, which would provide scholarship applicants with a simple application process and quick, easy access to needed information. First, applicants would be required to apply to universities concurrent with or prior to applying for scholarships, and scholarships would be contingent upon acceptance to eligible universities. This scheme would avoid the situation in which a student who is not admitted to a university receives a scholarship. Second, the application form, which could be filled out online, would be brief and consistent across scholarship programs. In addition, all scholarship guidelines would be clearly outlined and available online. Finally, scholarship recipient requests in matters such as a change of major would be handled promptly.

Flexibility. We know from our research that students wish for greater flexibility. Top-performing students and students who apply to the loan-based program would be awarded with greater flexibility in choosing countries and fields of study. The flexibility allowed under the prestigious program would ideally serve as an incentive for students to excel in secondary school.

Support. All Qatari residents, especially secondary students, would be given systematic guidance and assistance to make post-secondary decisions, including course of study, institution of study, country of study, and scholarship options. In addition, we proposed that all scholarship recipients receive guidance and support before, during, and immediately after their post-secondary studies. Scholarship recipients who choose to study abroad would receive comprehensive orientation before leaving Qatar. Scholarship recipients would also be aided by a coordinated buddy system, as well as by scholarship office staff members in Qatar.

Qatar's Education Reform Initiatives

The proposed scholarship system involves much more than guidelines for awarding scholarships; it could be an important part of Qatar's education reform strategy. The proposed system might encourage greater integration of secondary and post-secondary education through extensive student guidance and support, as well as through an integrated data system to monitor student performance over an extended period. It could also allow for a formal quality-assurance mechanism as new institutions are recruited for Education City. Most importantly, by encouraging students to attend the finest institutions worldwide, the system could also encourage the K–12 reforms currently under way that emphasize English-language learning and incorporate new curriculum standards and assessments. The K–12 and post-secondary reforms—taken together—might, over time, foster an educational culture that rewards academic achievement, motivates students to excel, and returns highly trained talent to Qatari society.

Implications for Policymakers

As mentioned, our recommendations were intended not just to improve the functioning of the scholarship programs. We also strove to recommend a system for Qatar that would align the scholarship programs with greater societal needs. The establishment of a new institute to oversee the post-secondary-education sector should ensure that resources are aligned in supporting post-secondary and foundational study for students domestically and abroad. This institute could conduct broad strategic planning for the post-secondary sector and evaluate component scholarship programs and other post-secondary programs to ensure alignment across them.

We hope that policymakers outside Qatar learn from this research as well. We advise that policymakers think broadly about societal needs in establishing scholarship programs. In addition to considering employment needs, it may also be important to develop gatekeepers of one's culture, such as historians, artists, musicians, and the like. In thinking about how to best prepare students for society, we recommend developing incentives to capitalize on the quality provided in the global marketplace while strengthening home campuses. For example, by requiring eligible institutions to be of higher quality than Qatar University, Qatar University has an incentive to maintain and improve its quality to sustain and grow its enrollment.

Another way to protect home campuses is to support and subsidize semesters abroad for those students who want exposure to another country. Finally, in considering incentives for students and institutions, it is important to consider how broader societal incentives for employment and other life choices would intersect with scholarship policies.

Possible Unintended Consequences

It is important to note that, considering the proposed stringent criteria for scholarship awards, it is possible that the number of scholarship recipients would decline in the short run from the roughly 8 percent of Qatari high-school graduates who had received a Ministry of Education scholarship to begin their undergraduate studies each year. The proposed plan assumes that most of the demand in the early years will be for precollege (for new secondary-school graduates) and study-abroad (for current post-secondary students) scholarships. Elevating award criteria is critical to system success in the long run, because it would ultimately help motivate applicants to excel in secondary school and gain admission to high-ranking institutions. Many of the scholarship recipients sponsored by the Ministry of Education and other employer scholarship programs received scholarships to study at low-ranked four-year institutions and community colleges. As scholarships were based largely on the results of the Qatari high-school exit exam, which is not correlated with any measure of aptitude or post-secondary entrance requirements, students had little incentive to excel in secondary school. The strict rules that could reduce the number of recipients in the short term should produce better outcomes in the long term, as students who want scholarships to support post-secondary education will need to earn them through academic achievement.

Because the prestigious scholarship is the most generous and the most flexible, it is possible that the best-performing students will gravitate toward this option. Further, it is possible that these students would select fields of study that are not aligned with workforce needs. Such choices could prevent employers from hiring the most talented Qataris. However, it is highly unlikely that there will be many students who are eligible for the prestigious scholarship, at least in the near term, given that only 6 percent of scholarship recipients were studying at highly selective institutions at the time of this study. In addition, there are extensive employment opportunities in the government sector, where Qataris are basically guaranteed employment. Furthermore, if students are aware of future employment options and salaries, many will choose majors that will allow them to compete for high-paying employment positions.

It is more likely that most students will select the employer-sponsored program. This scenario may seem to offer less choice to students than did the old scholarship system, under which the employer programs attracted fewer students than the Ministry of Education programs. However, it is important to note that, under the old system, the Ministry of Education provided scholarships only to students pursuing specified majors based on employer needs. Therefore, even if most students in the new system select the employer-sponsored program, the addition of prestigious and loan-based programs allow for choice that was more constrained under the old system.

Establishing the Higher Education Institute

The SEC accepted these recommendations and established the HEI in September 2004 with a similar organizational structure to the proposed PEI. Specifically, the HEI houses a scholarship office, institutional standards office, and an advising and career center, each with roles and responsibilities similar to those outlined in Chapter Five. The goals and guiding principles as outlined in Chapter Two serve as the basis for the HEI.

Starting with the recommendations in our report, the HEI developed five new scholarship programs: the Emiri Scholarship, National Scholarship, Employee Scholarship, Diploma Scholarship, and Pre-College Grant programs. The Emiri Scholarship, Employee Scholarship, and Pre-College Grant programs are similar to the prestigious, employer-based, and precollege grant programs outlined in Chapter Four. In addition, the HEI offers numerous opportunities for students to study abroad. The National Scholarship program was added by the HEI for students with the potential to become future business and professional leaders in targeted fields in Qatar. The Diploma Scholarship program was added for students seeking technical or specialized diplomas in such fields as nursing and aviation. A loan-based scholarship program, as outlined in Chapter Four, is under consideration for non-Qataris to study at select high-quality institutions and may be implemented in the near future.

For more information on the organizational structure of the HEI in Qatar and scholarship programs discussed here, see SEC (2008). It is clear that the HEI has transformed our ideas and suggestions, and its continual improvements demonstrate that it is responsive to the need to change. Further research could determine the extent to which specific recommendations, such as those related to student-support services or incentives designed to encourage students to excel academically, were adopted and which ones have worked better in practice than others. Such a study could further guide other countries in their attempts to balance support for internal post-secondary systems with support for study-abroad opportunities.

APPENDIX A

Survey of Selected Scholarship Programs

This appendix details model employer-sponsored, government-sponsored, and prestigious scholarship programs. Table A.1 presents employer-sponsored and government-sponsored scholarship programs, and Table A.2 presents prestigious scholarship programs. For the employer-sponsored programs, we chose to focus on large U.S. companies with highly selective programs and companies that resemble those in Qatar (e.g., oil companies). For the prestigious programs, we selected U.S. and UK programs that are highly selective and have had a long history of operation. For each of the scholarship programs, we examined such program features as the target population, acceptance criteria, student orientation and support services, country and program of study, flexibility, and financial awards. These scholarship programs informed the design of our proposed Qatar scholarship system, as well as the specific features of the individual scholarship programs.

Table A.1
Corporate- and Government-Sponsored Scholarship Programs

		Corporate Programs					Government Agency Programs	
	Requirement	**Cisco Systems**	**Microsoft**	**Boeing**	**Shell, Centenary Scholarship Fund**	**Walt Disney Company**	**NIH**	**NASA, National Space Grant College and Fellowship Program**
Purpose	Leadership					X		
	Contribution to society		X		X	X	X	X
	Meets HR needs	X	X	X		X	X	X
Target pop.	Undergraduate	X	X	X		X	X	X
	Graduate	X			X			X
Acceptance criteria	Leadership, entrepreneurial achievements				X	X		
	Certain GPA, test score, or class quartile	>3.2 GPA	>3.0 GPA	>3.0 GPA			>3.5 GPA or top 5%	
	Previous degree	Currently enrolled in an undergrad program	Currently enrolled in an undergrad program	Currently enrolled in an undergrad program	X			
	Requires nomination	X						
	U.S. citizen	X		X	Citizen of a non-OECD country	X	X	X
	Minority	X	In two of three offered scholarships				X	
	Age				(generally) <35			

Table A.1—Continued

		Corporate Programs					Government Agency Programs	
	Requirement	**Cisco Systems**	**Microsoft**	**Boeing**	**Shell, Centenary Scholarship Fund**	**Walt Disney Company**	**NIH**	**NASA, National Space Grant College and Fellowship Program**
Scholarship details	Number of students accepted	8	100+	9 (3 sophomore, 3 junior, 3 senior)	At least 65	1	15	
	Number of applicants	?	500–700	?	"Growing number of applicants"	?	Highly competitive	Highly competitive
	Timeline from acceptance to announcement	March–April	January–March	April–May	February–August	February–April	February–June	?
	Orientation				X ("welcome event" in October)			
	Support services				Universities offer student support			
Flexibility and choice	Institution	Cisco Systems–approved universities	X	Boeing-approved universities	Cambridge, Durham, Edinburgh, Oxford	X	X	X
	Area of study	Computer science	Computer science	Aerospace science	Int'l development (flexible)	Business administration or fine arts	Health sciences	Sciences and engineering
	Country of study	USA	USA, Canada, Mexico	USA	UK	X	X	USA
	Duration	X	1 year	1 year	1 year	4 years	1 year, renewable	1–3 years
Financial benefits	Partial tuition	1 year, $2,500		1 year, $10,000				X
	Full tuition		1 year		X	X	1 year, $20,000	
	Living expenses				X	$200	X	X
	Travel expenses				X			
	Research							

Table A.1—Continued

		Corporate Programs					Government Agency Programs	
	Requirement	Cisco Systems	Microsoft	Boeing	Shell, Centenary Scholarship Fund	Walt Disney Company	NIH	NASA, National Space Grant College and Fellowship Program
Employment	Sponsor organization employment		X					
	Sector employment	Electrical engineering and computer science	Technical fields	Aerospace industry			Biomedical and health-related research	
	Sponsor organization summer internship		Salaried internship of 12 weeks at Microsoft				Salaried internship of 10 weeks (each year) in NIH labs	
	Sector summer internship							
Obligations	Loan						Loan repayment programs, up to $35,000	
	Postgraduation seminars or programs						50% research effort for two years	
	Penalty for incompletion				Only one student did not complete the course (no penalty)		?	

NOTE: "X" indicates a requirement. NIH = National Institutes of Health. OECD = Organization for Economic Co-Operation and Development.

Table A.2
Prestigious Scholarship Programs

		Programs					
	Requirement	**British Marshall**	**Fulbright**	**Gates Cambridge**	**Rhodes**	**Rotary**	**Truman**
Purpose	Leadership	X	X	X	X	X	X
	Contribution to society	X	X	X	X	X	X
	Meets HR needs						
Target pop.	Undergraduate					X	
	Graduate	X	X (in some countries, formal graduate study is not required)	X	X	X	X
Acceptance criteria	Leadership, entrepreneurial achievements	X	X	X	X	X	Public service leadership
	Certain GPA, test score, or class quartile	>3.7 GPA			>3.4 GPA		>3.4 GPA
	Previous degree	X	X	X	X	X	X
	U.S. citizen	X	X				X
	Requires nomination				X	X	X
	Age	<26	<30		18–24		

Table A.2—Continued

		Programs					
	Requirement	British Marshall	Fulbright	Gates Cambridge	Rhodes	Rotary	Truman
Scholarship details	Number of students accepted	40	1,000 U.S. students and 1,400 foreign students	40–60	32	1,100–1,200	75–80
	Number of applicants	850–900	4,500	5,300	?	10,000–11,000	600
	Timeline from acceptance to announcement	October–February	October–February	November–March	October–December	Timeline differs by program	Early January–late March, junior year
	Orientation	Induction week in London in May (other organized events follow throughout the year)	No formal orientation	?	Group orientation at Oxford prior to the first semester	Students meet with local Rotary club members and a "sponsor counselor"	Mandatory weeklong leadership training in May (focusing on choice of study, teamwork, policy issues)
	Support services	British Marshall secretariat aids scholars in the UK	U.S. and abroad Fulbright offices	?	?	Rotary club "sponsor counselor"	Truman Foundation
Flexibility and choice	Institution	X	X	Cambridge	Oxford	X	X
	Area of study	X (in 2001, 29 science and 59 arts)	X	X	X	X	Public policy study encouraged
	Country of study	UK	X	UK	UK	X	X
	Duration	2 years	2–3 years	1–4 years	2–3 years	1 year	2–3 years

Table A.2—Continued

	Requirement	British Marshall	Fulbright	Gates Cambridge	Rhodes	Rotary	Truman
		Programs					
Financial benefits	Partial tuition					X	
	Full tuition	£20,000	X	X	X		$30,000
	Living expenses	X	X	X	X	X	X
	Travel expenses	X	X	X	X	X	X
	Research	X	X	X	X		X
Employment	Sponsor organization employment						
	Sector employment						Public service strongly encouraged
	Sponsor organization summer internship						The Brookings Institution and Truman Foundation
	Sector summer internship						8-week summer internship (public policy lab) in Washington, D.C.
Obligations	Loan	None	None	None	None	None	None
	Postgraduation seminars or programs	None	None	None	None	Alumni associations worldwide	None
	Penalty for incompletion	The Marshall Commission holds the discretion to act if a scholar fails to complete degree during a 2-year tenure. This is very rare.	None	?	?	Scholar will not receive a certificate of completion and may owe money to the Rotary Foundation	None

NOTE: "X" indicates a requirement.

APPENDIX B

Scholarship Programs in Countries with Similarities to Qatar

This appendix provides information on scholarship programs in countries with similarities to Qatar in terms of population, per capita GDP, domestic education, labor demands, and economic base. We chose small, high-income countries that are similar to Qatar to the extent that they do not have well-developed domestic higher-education systems but do have growing economies that demand increasing numbers of skilled workers. After providing general information on the scholarship programs in six such countries in Table B.1, we provide more detailed information on Singapore's highly regarded scholarship system based on a site visit there. Singapore and Qatar are both very affluent countries and are relatively similar in area and population. Both also rely on government-sponsored scholarships to ensure access to high-quality post-secondary institutions. The country scholarship systems outlined here informed both the design of our proposed scholarship system and the specific features of the individual scholarship programs.

Table B.1
Scholarship Programs in Countries with Similarities to Qatar

Country	Population	Per Capita GDP ($)	Domestic Education Institutions and Characteristics	Labor Demands and Economy	Some Scholarship Details
Brunei	358,098	18,600	1 university, 2 state-run teacher-training colleges, 6 technical schools	Oil and gas account for approx. 40% of GDP and 90% of export earnings. Recent emphasis on diversification, developing human resources (engineering, computer science, pharmacy, and biomedical science)	If a university course is not available in Brunei, the government supports students to study abroad. Ministry of education approves universities abroad for which it recognizes degrees and has "scholarship and training unit." Joint programs with University of Queensland Twinning programs with overseas universities Education loans through HSBC; ministry reimburses based on performance Some private-sector scholarships are contingent on postgrad employment (e.g., Baiduri Bank, Brunei Shell Co., Brunei LNG Co.).
Hong Kong	7,394,170	26,000	8 public universities Government mission to provide education irrespective of financial means General perception that best students go abroad Recent focus on recruiting mainland talent	Financial and banking center, developed human capital and resources	Means-tested tuition assistance to needy full-time students (grant or loan) Private-sector and foundation-supported scholarships (e.g., Hang Seng Bank) Some specific scholarships for students entering agricultural and marine industries and students committed to Hong Kong's development
Malaysia	23,092,340	9,300	Numerous public and private universities	Large industrial base (tin mining, manufacturing, construction) Other important sectors are semiconductors, natural rubber, agriculture, and tourism Emphasis on science, engineering, IT, and communication	Scholarships through ministry of science, technology, and environment (science-related courses at local universities or abroad) Study abroad allowed only if courses not available domestically Ministry provides approximately 100 scholarships per year Scholarships offered through central bank (Bank Negara), as well as loans and financial aid (public service department loan scheme) Universities may waive/decrease fees based on performance Private-sector scholarships (e.g., HSBC, Caltex) available
Oman	2,807,125 (including 577,293 ex-pats)	8,300	1 private university, 2 public university/college, 18 private colleges Emphasis on recruiting foreign students to study in Oman	Emphasis on diversification of sectors other than oil Concentration on developing human resources and nation's gas resources, creating jobs for youth, and "Omanization" (like Qatarization) Economy improved considerably in 2000 due to the upturn in oil prices	Scholarships through ministry of education, ministry of higher education, and ministry of labor Government funds nearly half of undergrads studying at private colleges and universities Partial scholarships are offered based on secondary-school certificate exams and/or country of study Other opportunities through Education and Culture Committee, Bahwan Engineering Company, Petroleum Development Oman, and Natural Gas Company Scholarships allocated based on labor-market needs

Table B.1—Continued

Country	Population	Per Capita GDP ($)	Domestic Education Institutions and Characteristics	Labor Demands and Economy	Some Scholarship Details
Qatar	817,052 (including approx. 600,000 ex-pats)	21,500	1 public university, 1 private medical school, 1 private community college Education City, consisting of several private universities, recently opened	Oil accounts for more than 30% of GDP, roughly 80% of export earnings, and 58% of government revenues Natural-gas reserves are third largest in the world Paucity of Qataris to fill leadership and management positions Emphasis on training Qataris in engineering, IT, communication, medicine, and nursing	Scholarships through Ministry of Education, other ministries and quasiprivate-sector companies (Qatar Petroleum, Q-Tel) for undergraduate and graduate study abroad Sponsor may support students for bridge or foundation year at home or abroad Ministry of Education must approve study abroad Scholarships allocated based on labor-market needs Nearly all scholarships granted with bond or postgraduate employment commitment
Singapore	4,608,595	24,700	3 public universities; 2 strong in engineering, biosciences General perception that UK and U.S. universities are superior to domestic ones Singapore is trying to improve domestic universities to become a regional "education hub" Families can afford domestic universities but not universities overseas	Heavily dependent on human capital and human resources Major Asian financial hub Prominent sectors include banking, electronics, petroleum refining and petrochemicals, and machinery Emphasis on life sciences, biotech, and engineering	Most scholarships administered through PSC for undergraduate and graduate (master's) studies; very little support for Ph.D. study Government allocates scholarships based on labor-market projections (assessment based on survey of ministries and government agencies) and student merit Scholarship recipients encouraged and groomed from first year in high school Nearly all scholarships granted with bond; some choice in postgrad employment Employers grant a small number of scholarships annually
Thailand	64,265,276	6,900		Heavily reliant on export-led growth and highly developed manufacturing sector, especially in high-tech goods Economy not developed enough to utilize high-tech skills gained abroad Government allocates scholarships based on labor-market needs	Most scholarships administered by office of civil service, but individual ministries also have own programs Exams and interviews required for scholarships More graduate scholarships than undergraduate A few private-sector scholarships (e.g., Intel Microelectronics) available Nearly all scholarships granted with bond

SOURCE: CIA (2003).

NOTE: PSC = Singapore Public Service Commission.

Singapore's Scholarship Programs

Why Study Singapore?

Our comparative study focused on Singapore for the following reasons:

- Singapore and Qatar have similar population sizes.
- Singapore and Qatar are very affluent countries.
- Singapore and Qatar are proportional to each other in size.
- Singapore sends many students abroad on government-sponsored scholarships.

Table B.2 compares relevant characteristics of Qatar and Singapore.

What Did We Find?

Singapore's goal is to be the education hub of Southeast Asia. Thus, the government subsidizes higher education in various ways, including financing students to study abroad at prestigious universities.[1]

Broadly speaking, scholarships are awarded by three bodies:

- the PSC
- employers (e.g., Singapore Air, DBS Bank, Temasek Holdings)
- FIREfly Alliance (a coalition of seven boards and ministries).

The Public Service Commission

The PSC is a body of 70 staff members that administers government scholarships. Its vision is to be the leading scholarship authority in Singapore, and finances the bulk of Singapore's scholarships. Its functions include

- promoting and marketing commission scholarships
- selecting scholarship recipients
- supporting scholars during their time abroad

Table B.2
Comparison of Qatar and Singapore

Characteristic	Qatar	Singapore
Population	817,052 (July 2003 est.)	4,608,595 (July 2003 est.)
Population growth rate (%)	2.87 (2003 est.)	3.42 (2003 est.)
Geographic area (sq km)	11,437	692.7
GDP ($)	17.2 billion (2002 est.)	105 billion (2002 est.)
Per capita GDP ($)	21,500 (2002 est.)	24,000 (2002 est.)
Government scholarships awarded	216 (2003)	74 (2002)
Students abroad	1,222 (2001/2002)	~500 (2002/2003)

SOURCE: CIA (2003).

[1] Prestigious universities are, roughly, the top 10 universities in every country.

- developing policies and programs to help the scholar reach his or her fullest potential
- providing career guidance to scholars upon graduation
- assessing ministry staffing needs.

Because government-sponsored scholarships are the most prestigious in Singapore, the PSC receives more than 900 applications annually and awards fewer than 80 scholarships. The detailed selection system includes (1) an examination of A-level results and other grades, (2) interviews, (3) personality examinations, and (4) examination of extracurricular activities.

The PSC offers five different types of awards, based on students' abilities, choice of major or career, and Singapore's labor-market needs:

- the President's Scholarship
- Overseas Merit Scholarship
- Local-Overseas Merit Scholarship
- Singapore Armed Forces Overseas Scholarship
- Singapore Police Force Overseas Scholarship.

The President's Scholarship is the most prestigious and the most competitive undergraduate scholarship in Singapore. Scholarships are awarded annually to students who have outstanding academic results, demonstrated leadership qualities, and an enthusiasm to serve the nation. Scholars may study any course leading to a degree at a local or overseas university. President's Scholarships are generally awarded concurrently with another PSC scholarship.

PSC scholarships are often tied to a specific ministry, so when the scholar returns, he or she must work for that ministry (e.g., defense or education). Alternatively, a student may study on an "open" scholarship that would allow him or her to work in any government agency. About 35 open scholarships are awarded each year. The scholarships offer roughly the same financial packages, varying only by university costs. The following are some of the requirements and policies:

- The scholarships can be used for undergraduate studies at universities in Singapore, the United States, the United Kingdom, France, Germany, Japan, Canada, and Australia.
- Students propose fields of study and institutions. The area of study is generally flexible.
- Selected scholarships can be used for a master's degree course (with PSC approval).
- Scholars are provided with full scholarship and air passage. On graduation, they are required to serve a bond of four to six years.
- Scholars sign a detailed contract with a repayment plan that specifies costs that must be reimbursed if the student drops out at any point.
- Students are given only four years to study abroad.

Employer Scholarships

While in Singapore, we met with four private employers: Temasek Holdings, DBS Bank, Singapore Air, and the Inter-Comm Development Authority.

There are no centralized policies governing the private-employer scholarship system. However, there is informal collusion among employers. Generally speaking, all the employers maintain the same conditions, benefits, and regulations as the PSC (so that student decisions are not based on the scholarship's financial rewards). This includes length of stay, bonds, universities, countries, and areas of study. Private employers generally offer only one to 10 scholarships per year. Scholars are not provided with a salary while studying but are required to serve a bond with the sponsor company upon return. The bonds are shorter for students who study at local universities.

FIREfly Alliance Scholarships

FIREfly is a human resource alliance of seven agencies (or statutory boards) under Singapore's Ministry of Trade and Industry.[2] The seven agencies have come together to attract, develop, and retain talent. As part of the FIREfly initiative, the seven agencies no longer offer scholarships on an individual basis—but, rather, as a group. While in Singapore, we met with the largest of these agencies, the Economic Development Board.

FIREfly scholarships are unique in several ways:

- The alliance jointly markets, recruits, designs guidelines, and develops performance criteria.
- While a student can apply to any preferred agency under the FIREfly umbrella, his or her application will be considered by all seven agencies.
- The parent agency (the agency within FIREfly that sponsors a particular student) has the authority to determine what its scholars will study.
- Upon return to Singapore, a scholar can rotate jobs among the agencies after completing two years with the parent agency.

---

[2] These include the Agency for Science, Technology, and Research; Economic Development Board; Energy Market Authority; International Enterprise Singapore; JTC Corporation; Standard Productivity and Innovation Board; and Singapore Tourism Board.

APPENDIX C

Sample of Interview Protocols

Scholarship Recipient: Interview Questions Regarding Qatari Higher-Education Scholarship Programs

Background Questions

Tell us about your family's background (education level of parents and siblings, any other scholarship recipients in the family).

Over what period did you receive a scholarship?

What degree program or major did you pursue with the scholarship? At what university?

What is your current employment?

Mission and Objective of Scholarship Program

What do you think should be the primary mission and objectives of the scholarship program? What should the program promote?

In practice, is the program meeting these objectives? If yes, how? If no, how would you suggest changing the program to meet these objectives?

Is the scholarship program helping to meet labor-market demands in Qatar? Is the program contributing to social and economic development in Qatar?

Application and Acceptance Process

How did you learn about the scholarship program?

Why did you decide to apply? Why did you want to study abroad or study at a university with instruction in English?

How did you decide where to study (both country and institution)? How did you decide on a graduate program or major? Is the Ministry of Education involved in this decisionmaking process? Who do you think should be involved in the decision to choose a country, institution, and major? (For example, should this be up to students alone or to policymakers, for example?)

Please describe the scholarship program application process (e.g., materials you submitted, interaction with Ministry of Education).

Were there any barriers or delays in the application process? If yes, how would you recommend improving the process?

Do you think that the scholarship selection criteria are sufficient? Are there additional criteria that you think should be included in the selection process?

Academic Bridge Program

[Questions posed to current scholarship recipients only, as the Academic Bridge Program is only two years old.]

Please describe your experience with the Academic Bridge Program. Must all scholarship recipients go through the Academic Bridge Program? If not, what criteria are used in referring scholarship recipients to the Academic Bridge Program?

When, during the course of the Academic Bridge Program, do scholarship recipients apply to universities?

What type of counseling, if any, do Academic Bridge Program students receive in selecting and applying to English-language universities? If they receive counseling, is the Ministry of Education involved?

Did the Academic Bridge Program adequately prepare you to study abroad (or for universities with English instruction in Qatar)? Is there anything you would have liked to have learned through the Academic Bridge Program but did not? Could the program be improved in any way? If yes, how?

University Experience

Is there any sort of orientation program or event for scholarship recipients studying abroad? If no, do you think that such an event would be useful to recipients?

Please describe your interaction with cultural attachés. Did they play any role in advising you about universities, various programs or majors? What type of interaction or contact did you or do you have with cultural attachés during your course of study? What types of communication did you or do you have with the Ministry of Education during your course of study? Do you see a need for more or less interaction or communication with cultural attachés and the Ministry of Education during the course of study? Why?

What type of interaction or contact did you or do you have with other scholarship recipients during your course of study (e.g., phone, email, living together, studying together, socializing)? How often did you or do you interact with other Qatari students studying abroad in the same country? Is/was contact information for scholarship recipients studying abroad available to you?

Please describe your experience abroad or at a university with instruction in English. What did you like about the university and studying abroad? What did you dislike?

Do you feel that you were adequately prepared (academically, socially, culturally) for your course of study? If yes, what prepared you? If no, how could you have been better prepared?

Did you have any access to in-country counseling (e.g., advice about course of study, adjusting to new lifestyle)? If no, would you have benefited from this kind of counseling?

Do recipients receive any in-country support if academic performance is poor (e.g., tutoring, additional English instruction)? If no, would recipients benefit from this kind of support?

Did you or do you have any experience with scholarship recipients who dropped out of school? If so, please provide profiles of the students (e.g., why they dropped out, gender, academic background, where they studied, what they did after dropping out).

After Graduation

What type of interaction or contact did you or do you have with cultural attachés or Ministry of Education representatives upon receiving your degree? Did you discuss career goals or employment options with them? Do scholarship recipients tell Ministry of Education officials or cultural attachés where they would like to work? Do they start submitting job applications before graduation? Did Ministry of Education officials have any influence over your location or sector of employment? If no, would you like the ministry to play a role in where scholarship recipients are employed? Would you have benefited from more or different kinds of interaction after graduation?

Where were you employed upon finishing your degree? How did you find this job?

How was your course of study related to your first job and your current job?

Is there anything that you would have liked to have learned at university but did not (e.g., something that could have better prepared you for your career)?

Recommendations

Overall, were you or are you satisfied with the scholarship program?

What are the primary advantages of the scholarship program? What do you like most about it?

What aspects of the program need improvement? What are the program's shortcomings?

If you could restructure the scholarship program in any way, how would you do it?

Is there anything else you would like to tell us?

Ministry of Education Protocol: Interview Questions Regarding Qatari Higher-Education Scholarship Programs

Background Questions

How long have you been involved with the scholarship program?

Mission and Objectives

What do you think should be the primary mission and objectives of the scholarship program? What should the program promote?

How close is the reality to your opinion of what the program's mission and purpose should be? If it is not close, how would you suggest changing the program to meet its objectives?

Do you think scholarship program recipients are going to the "right" institutions?

Do you think the scholarship program is helping to meet labor-market demands in Qatar? Is the program contributing to social and economic progress in Qatar? Are these two goals mutually exclusive, or do you see one as more important or urgent than the other?

Selection and Application Procedures

[Questions posed to scholarship committee staff only.]

Last time we spoke with Scholarship Office staff, we were told about the current selection criteria: 550 TOEFL score, two years of civil service (for graduate studies), minimum GPA, and minimum score on the high-school exit exam. We learned that the "minimum" levels change every year. Could you tell us what the minimum levels are this year? Why do they change from year to year? Is there a strategy or rationale behind these changes (e.g., political pressure to admit some students, budget)?

Do you think these selection criteria are sufficient? Are there any additional criteria that you would like to include in the selection process? (We have heard suggestions of educational or workplace performance.)

We obtained information about the number of acceptances for the program (80 out of 150 at the undergraduate level; 50 out of slightly more than 50 at the graduate level). Why were certain applicants not accepted?

How many applicants accept the scholarship after being notified that they will receive funding through the scholarship program? Is this different for males and females? Students from private schools and students from government schools?

Please describe the materials required in applying to the scholarship program. What materials do you require applicants to submit? (For example, letters of recommendation, personal statements, and so on.) [Ask for a copy of the application form.] Are there any additional materials that you would like to see applicants submit?

When is the deadline for scholarship applications?

How much time is there between when applicants submit applications and when they receive notice? And when they receive funding? Ideally, how long do you think the application process should take? [If the reply is that it should be faster, ask for suggestions on how to speed up the process.]

Do applicants specify what they plan to study or their planned major in the application? Do applicants specify where they would like to study?

How do students/applicants decide where (host country, academic institution) and what (major, degree program) to study? Is the Ministry of Education involved in this decisionmaking process? If not, who is?

Does the Ministry of Education have a preference for where or what recipients study (i.e., host country or academic institution, major)? Should anyone be involved in the students' decision-making process?

In terms of scholarship sponsors (for masters and doctoral programs), how does the sponsorship system work? Do sponsors have any influencing over students' decisions about majors? Do sponsors decide majors or other aspects? Can students get scholarships for graduate studies without being nominated or having a sponsor?

Program Details

We've heard that all students are legally required to go to the Academic Bridge Program before studying abroad. Is this true? Must all scholarship recipients go through the program? [Probe for undergraduate and graduate, English and Arabic universities, English-instruction universities in Doha (e.g., Cornell).] What proportion of scholarship recipients planning to study at universities with English instruction attends the Academic Bridge Program?

Financial Issues

Do you ask for any financial information from applicants? Do scholarship recipients come from families that could afford to send children abroad to study? Is the scholarship program assisting families that could not afford to send children abroad to study? [In other words, is the program based on need?]

We've been told—and have seen statistics that show—that many students go on to study abroad with their own funds. Why would someone study abroad without going through the scholarship program? We understand that the Ministry of Education sometimes starts funding these students in the middle of their programs of study. Why would it want to support these students, too?

How do recipients receive funding (for living expenses, clothes, books, etc.)? How do host institutions receive funding (for tuition, health insurance, dormitory, etc.)?

For how many years will the Ministry of Education support a scholarship recipient? For example, if an undergraduate takes longer than average to complete a degree, will the ministry continue to support him or her? For how many years will the ministry support scholarship recipients for graduate study?

Do graduate scholarship recipients who are sponsored by a ministry or company still receive their salary while they are studying abroad?

Is there a maximum amount of money that the Ministry of Education is willing to spend on the scholarship program? How much is the annual budget for the scholarship program? Is there a "quota" of how many scholarships should be given each year (e.g., does the budget have to be exhausted)? Does the program have a goal for the number of scholarships given each year?

If there is a quota or a maximum number of scholarships given each year, how does the selection committee prioritize among sponsors for the graduate scholarships (i.e., are there any set quotas or numbers of scholarships that have to be assigned each year by type of sponsorship: private sponsors, ministry sponsors, and so on)? How does the selection committee decide how many undergraduate and how many graduate scholarships to award?

Does the Ministry of Education consider cost when allocating scholarships? For example, are recipients encouraged to study wherever they choose? Should recipients be encouraged to study wherever they choose?

Other Operational Issues

Is there any sort of orientation program or event for scholarship recipients studying abroad? If not, do you think such an event would be useful to recipients?

Student Performance and Experiences Abroad

What information do you collect on student performance (e.g., performance reviews, grades)? What additional information, if any, would you like to have on student performance?

Communication

How frequent is communication between the Ministry of Education and the cultural attachés? Do you see a need for more or less communication? Why?

What type of communication occurs between recipients and the Ministry of Education? Is contact information for scholarship recipients studying abroad available to them?

Student Support Services

Do recipients receive any in-country support (outside of the university) if academic performance is poor (e.g., tutoring, additional English instruction)? Would recipients benefit from this kind of support?

Do recipients have access to any in-country counseling (e.g., advice about course of study, help adjusting to new lifestyle)? Would recipients benefit from this kind of counseling?

Dropouts

What information do you collect on scholarship recipients who drop out of school?

Are dropout rates different for recipients studying in English-speaking versus Arabic-speaking countries? Is this different for graduates and undergraduates? Is this different for males and females? By year of study? (For example, do most who drop out leave in the beginning of their studies or toward the end?)

Do you have any contact information for recipients who have dropped out? (Would it be interesting for us to talk with one or two of them?)

After Graduation

Communication

Please describe the relationship between scholarship recipients and the Ministry of Education after students graduate. How does the ministry follow up with recipients? [If there is no follow-up, ask what the ministry would like to know about recipients after they have graduated.]

What type of communication occurs between the Ministry of Education or cultural attachés and scholarship recipients after graduation?

Postgraduation Employment

Do scholarship recipients tell Ministry of Education officials or cultural attachés where they would like to work? Do they start submitting applications before graduation?

Do Ministry of Education officials have any influence over recipients' location or sector of employment? If no, would you like the ministry to play a role in where scholarship recipients are employed?

Do Ministry of Education representatives have a preference regarding where (i.e., what institutions or companies) recipients are employed? Who is involved in making this decision? Who should be involved?

Do Ministry of Education representatives discuss employment needs with counterparts from other ministries, government institutions, or private companies?

Academic Bridge Program

Do you feel that the Academic Bridge Program adequately prepares scholarship recipients to study abroad (or for universities with English instruction in Qatar)? [Asked of Ministry of Education officials and scholarship recipients:] Is there anything you would like scholarship recipients to learn through the Academic Bridge Program that they are not learning?

What does the program cost per year? Per student? [Get figures from Ministry of Education and Academic Bridge Program representatives.]

[Asked of Ministry of Education officials:] What type of financial support do scholarship recipients receive while enrolled in the Academic Bridge Program?

Employment of Scholarship Recipients

Please describe your experience with scholarship program recipients. How many scholarship recipients are currently employed at your organization? How did they apply for their current positions?

Have you ever nominated an employee for the scholarship program? If yes, how do you select employees to nominate for the scholarship program? What criteria do you use?

If you have nominated an employee, how did you learn about the scholarship program?

Please describe the nomination process (e.g., what paperwork you submitted, whom you talked to, anything else that was required).

Did you find the nomination process to be easy (not burdensome)? If no, what could be done to change the process? How could the process be improved?

If you nominate an employee, what type of guarantee do you have that the employee will return to your organization after receiving his or her degree?

After a former employee receives a degree, how is he or she reintegrated into your organization?

When recruiting scholarship recipients, how much do you value a diploma from a foreign university? If a student went abroad with a scholarship, does your perception of him or her improve? Does this make him or her more qualified?

How much do you value study in an English-speaking country? How do you value ability to speak English fluently?

When considering an applicant who has studied abroad, what matters more to you: country of study, university, or course of study?

Do you consider applicants' grades or GPA in hiring decisions?

Please describe profiles of applicants who would be ideally suited to work at your organization. What type of undergraduate major or graduate degrees would they have? What type of skills would they have? What languages would they speak?

Recommendations

Overall, are you or were you satisfied with the scholarship program?

What are the primary advantages of the scholarship program? What do you like most about it?

What aspects of the program need improvement? What are the program's shortcomings? If you could restructure the scholarship program in any way, how would you do it?

Do you think the scholarship program is sending an appropriate number of undergraduates (university students) abroad? Should it be sending more or fewer?

Do you think the scholarship program is sending an appropriate number of master's and doctoral students abroad? Should it be sending more or fewer?

Can you name institutions or universities abroad that you feel have good reputations?

Is there anything else you would like to tell us?

Data Requests

Do you have data on the number of applicants who accept or reject the scholarships by gender or other breakdowns (e.g., private school versus Ministry of Education school, by field of study)?

Do you have information about student performance (e.g., performance reviews, grades)?

Could you give us contact information through the cultural attachés for scholarship recipients in the primary countries in which they study (the United States, United Kingdom, Egypt, Saudi Arabia, Bahrain, and Jordan), including names, email addresses, phone numbers?

Do you have any data on dropouts from the program (e.g., gender, universities, majors)?

Do you have cost figures for the Academic Bridge Program? What does the program cost per year? Per student?

Qatar University Representatives: Interview Questions Regarding Qatari Higher-Education Scholarship Programs

Background Questions

Ask for

1. Title
2. How long he or she has been at Qatar University
3. Role.

Familiarity with Scholarship Program

How familiar are you with the scholarship program for Qatari students to pursue higher education? What do you know about it?

Are you personally involved with the scholarship program? How does your organization interact with it? Does Qatar University sponsor students for the program?

Do you see the scholarship program as a competitor for students (both undergraduate and graduate)? Why would students choose to study abroad as opposed to studying at Qatar University? Once enrolled in Qatar University, do students leave to study abroad?

Do students who do not successfully complete the Academic Bridge Program go to Qatar University?

Do you know how many students drop out of the scholarship program each year (e.g., at universities abroad) and enter Qatar University? Do you know why these students drop out? Are there any common reasons? Is there a common pattern? [Probe for issues related to gender, language, culture, etc.]

Mission and Objectives

What do you think should be the primary mission and objectives of the scholarship program? What should the program promote?

In practice, is the program meeting these objectives? If yes, how? If no, how would you suggest changing the program to meet these objectives?

Is the scholarship program helping to meet labor-market demands in Qatar? Is the program contributing to social and economic development in Qatar? Should it? If yes, how would you change the program to meet these objectives?

Questions Regarding Employees' and Potential Employees' Background and Skills

Do you encourage students interested in graduate study to apply to the scholarship program? Are all of these students sponsored? If no, how do you choose which students to sponsor?

Does Qatar University provide students with information about the scholarship program? Do students receive any assistance with applications? Does Qatar University give these only to the students it sponsors or to all students wishing to apply?

When recruiting faculty, how much do you value a diploma from a foreign university? If a student went abroad with a scholarship, does your perception of him or her improve? Does this make him or her more qualified?

How much do you value study in an English-speaking country? How do you value the ability to speak English fluently? Does this vary by department?

When considering an applicant who has studied abroad, what matters more to you: country of study, university, or course of study? [This may vary by department.]

Do you see the scholarship program as a useful source of faculty for Qatar University?

Are there any departments in which you have difficulty finding qualified faculty? If yes, do you use the scholarship program (by encouraging students to choose a certain major) to fill these shortages?

Do you think the scholarship program is sending students to the "right" institutions?

Can you name institutions or universities abroad that you feel have good reputations?

How could the scholarship program best meet the needs of Qatar University? How could the scholarship program ideally be tailored to your needs?

Would you mind referring us to professors who have been scholarship recipients?

Recommendations

Overall, are you or were you satisfied with the scholarship program?

What are the primary advantages of the scholarship program? What do you like most about it?

What aspects of the program need improvement? What are its shortcomings? If you could restructure the scholarship program in any way, how would you do it?

Do you think the scholarship program is sending an appropriate number of undergraduates (university students) abroad? Should it be sending more or fewer?

Do you think the scholarship program is sending an appropriate number of master's and doctoral students abroad? Should it be sending more or fewer?

Currently, the scholarship program uses a TOEFL score of 550, a minimum GPA, a minimum score on the high-school exit exam, and (for graduate studies) two years of civil service. Do you think that these selection criteria are sufficient? Are there additional criteria that you think should be included in the selection process?

Is there anything else you would like to tell us?

Data Requests

Do you collect information on Qatar University graduates who received scholarships to study abroad for graduate study? If yes, how many received scholarships through the Ministry of Education program? Where (country, institution) and what did they study?

What percent of Qatar University faculty have been scholarship recipients (or have studied abroad)? What is the breakdown by field (e.g., are there more recipients in engineering than in the humanities)?

Qatar Foundation: Interview Questions Regarding Qatari Higher-Education Scholarship Programs

Mission and Objectives

What do you think should be the primary mission and objectives of the scholarship program? What should the program promote? How much weight should labor-market needs be given in the design of a scholarship program?

Do you think the scholarship program is helping to meet labor-market demands in Qatar? Is the program contributing to social and economic progress? Are these two goals mutually exclusive, or do you see one as more important or urgent than the other?

Is cost an issue? Should the program be constrained by cost considerations?

Do you see the scholarships as a private good or a public good? Do you think that individuals or the country as a whole benefits the most?

How selective do you think this system should be in choosing students? How realistic is this, given the desperate need for certain occupations (for example, engineers and technicians)? Would you recommend that employers reward students (e.g., with higher salaries) for attending highly selective institutions, given that they are in desperate need of employees with specific skills?

Do you think that there are enough educational options in Qatar? Are there enough options for students who do not meet the criteria for scholarships? Should there be options for non-Qataris?

In general, how do the incentives in the scholarship program affect students' educational and employment choices (e.g., why study engineering abroad versus in Qatar, why go through the effort of going abroad when you can come back and earn the same salary)?

As a society, what does Qatar need from higher education? What are the benefits of getting this higher education in Arab countries? In Western countries? [Probe for cultural, attitudinal, behavioral changes.] Given these benefits, why should students attend institutions in Qatar? Do you think that the scholarship program should provide additional incentives for these students to go abroad? [Probe for whether the program should try to change gender roles.]

Should students be required to attend these in-country institutions if the majors are offered here?

Additional Questions

[If time permits.] What are the primary advantages of the scholarship program? What do you like most about it?

How close to reality is your opinion of what the program's mission and purpose should be? If you do not think they are close at all, what aspects of the program need improvement? What are its shortcomings? How would you suggest changing the program to meet its objectives?

Currently, the Ministry of Education uses high-school exit exam scores, TOEFL scores, and a record of civil service (for graduate programs) to assign scholarships. Do you think that the selection criteria are sufficient? Are there any additional criteria that you would like to include in the selection process?

Qatar Foundation as an Employer

Please describe profiles of applicants who would be ideally suited to working for your organization. What type of undergraduate major or graduate degrees would they have? What type of skills would they have? What languages would they speak?

Can you name institutions or universities abroad that you feel have good reputations?

Is there anything else you would like to tell us?

Academic Bridge Program: Interview Questions Regarding Qatari Higher-Education Scholarship Programs

Background Questions

Ask for

1. Title
2. How long he or she has been involved with the Academic Bridge Program
3. Role in the Academic Bridge Program
4. How he or she came to this position.

Familiarity with Scholarship Program

How familiar are you with the scholarship program for Qatari students to pursue higher education?

What is or has been your relationship to the scholarship program?

What do you think should be the primary mission and objectives of the scholarship program? What should the program promote?

In practice, is the program meeting these objectives? If yes, how? If no, how would you suggest changing the program to meet these objectives?

Is the scholarship program helping to meet labor-market demands in Qatar? Is the program contributing to social and economic development in Qatar?

Academic Bridge Program Details

Must all scholarship recipients go through the Academic Bridge Program? If not, what criteria are used in referring scholarship recipients to the program? Are there any individuals selected for the scholarship program but not admitted to the Academic Bridge Program?

Is the Academic Bridge Program required for all students planning to attend a university with English instruction (including universities with English instruction in Qatar)? For both undergraduate and graduate students? What proportion of scholarship recipients planning to study at universities with English instruction attends the Academic Bridge Program? Do students planning to attend a university with Arabic instruction abroad go through the program?

When, during the course of the Academic Bridge Program, do scholarship recipients apply to universities?

What type of counseling, if any, do Academic Bridge Program students receive in selecting and applying to English-language universities? If they receive counseling, is the Ministry of Education involved?

What course of study do scholarship recipients have to complete through the Academic Bridge Program before beginning their study abroad?

Do scholarship students have any interaction with the Academic Bridge Program during their study at universities or after graduation? If so, please describe the interactions.

Do you feel that the Academic Bridge Program adequately prepares scholarship recipients for study abroad (or for universities with English instruction in Qatar)? Is there anything you would like scholarship recipients to learn through the Academic Bridge Program that they are not learning? Do you think the program should be reformed in any way? If yes, how would you change it?

What does the program cost per year? Per student?

What type of financial support do scholarship recipients receive while enrolled in the Academic Bridge Program?

Recommendations

Overall, are you satisfied with the scholarship program?

What are the primary advantages of the scholarship program? What do you like most about it?

What aspects of the program need improvement? What are the program's shortcomings?

If you could restructure the scholarship program in any way, how would you do it?

Is there anything else you would like to tell us?

APPENDIX D

Interviewees

Table D.1
Interviewee Information

Interviewee Affiliation	Location	Number of Interviewees
Supreme Education Council	Qatar	1
Academic Bridge Program	Qatar	1
Weill Cornell Medical School	Qatar	1
Hamad Medical Corporation	Qatar	2
Qatar University	Qatar	6
Center for Judicial and Legal Studies	Qatar	3
College of the North Atlantic	Qatar	1
Kahramaa	Qatar	2
Ministry of Foreign Affairs	Qatar	1
Ministry of Civil Services	Qatar	1
Ministry of Education Scholarship Office	Qatar	5
Ministry of Interior	Qatar	3
Planning Council	Qatar	2
Qatar Armed Forces	Qatar	2
Qatar Foundation	Qatar	4
Qatar Petroleum	Qatar	3
Q-Tel	Qatar	1
Ministry of Education scholarship recipient	United States	5
Ministry of Education scholarship recipient	United Kingdom	3
Employer-sponsored scholarship recipient	United States	6
Hybrid program scholarship recipient	United Kingdom	2
Cultural attaché's office	United States	1
Cultural attaché's office	United Kingdom	1
Private companies providing student-support services	United States	1
Other scholarship programs	Singapore	5
Total		63

References

Barron's Guide to the Most Competitive Colleges, New York: Barron's Educational Series, 2001.

Brewer, Dominic J., Catherine Augustine, Gail L. Zellman, Gery Ryan, Charles A. Goldman, Cathleen Stasz, and Louay Constant, *Education for a New Era: Design and Implementation of K–12 Education Reform in Qatar*, Santa Monica, Calif.: RAND Corporation, MG-548-QATAR, 2007. As of February 19, 2008: http://www.rand.org/pubs/monographs/MG548/

Central Intelligence Agency, *The World Factbook, 2003*, Washington, D.C.: U.S. Government Printing Office, 2003.

———, *The World Factbook, 2007*, Washington, D.C.: U.S. Government Printing Office, 2007.

CIA—*see* Central Intelligence Agency.

EducationGuardian, *The Guardian University Guide*, 2003. Data for 2004–2008 available, as of February 19, 2008:
http://education.guardian.co.uk/universityguide/

Qatar University, "QU Statistics," undated Web page. As of March 18, 2008:
http://www.qu.edu.qa/html/qustats.html

———, "The Reform Plan," Web page, 2006. As of February 19, 2008:
http://www.qu.edu.qa/html/reformplan.html

SEC—*see* Supreme Education Council.

Stasz, Cathleen, Eric Eide, and Francisco Martorell, with Louay Constant, Charles A. Goldman, Joy S. Moini, Vazha Nadareighvili, and Hanine Salem, *Post-Secondary Education in Qatar: Employer Demand, Student Choice, and Options for Policy*, Santa Monica, Calif.: RAND Corporation, MG-644-QATAR, 2007. As of February 19, 2008:
http://www.rand.org/pubs/monographs/MG644/

Supreme Education Council, Higher Education Institute, homepage, 2008. As of February 19, 2008:
http://www.english.education.gov.qa/section/sec/hei